COAST TO COAST

STUDENT'S BOOK 1

Jeremy Harmer and Harold Surguine

London and New York

Contents

Note: Interactions extending the oral practice for each unit are to be found on pages 72–91. A card mask is provided with this book, which students should use to cover their partner's information in information gap exercises.

The following symbols are used in the interactions:

pairwork
groupwork
whole class activity
teamwork

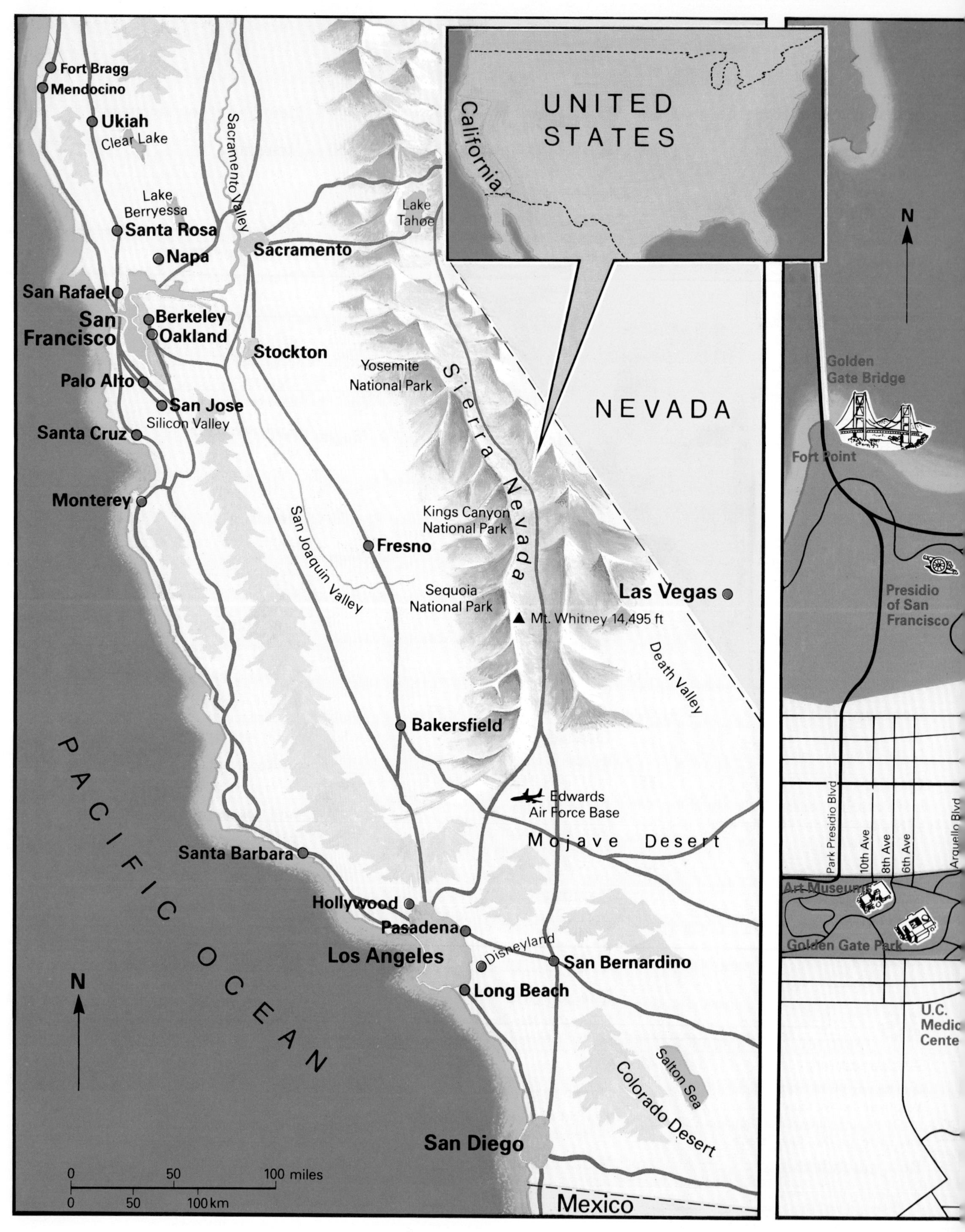

UNITED STATES
California
NEVADA
Fort Bragg
Mendocino
Ukiah
Clear Lake
Lake Berryessa
Sacramento Valley
Santa Rosa
Napa
Sacramento
Lake Tahoe
San Rafael
San Francisco
Berkeley
Oakland
Stockton
Palo Alto
San Jose
Silicon Valley
Santa Cruz
Monterey
Yosemite National Park
Sierra Nevada
Kings Canyon National Park
San Joaquin Valley
Fresno
Sequoia National Park
Las Vegas
Mt. Whitney 14,495 ft
Death Valley
Bakersfield
PACIFIC OCEAN
Edwards Air Force Base
Mojave Desert
Santa Barbara
Hollywood
Pasadena
Los Angeles
Disneyland
San Bernardino
Long Beach
Salton Sea
Colorado Desert
San Diego
Mexico
N
0 50 100 miles
0 50 100 km
Golden Gate Bridge
Fort Point
Presidio of San Francisco
Park Presidio Blvd
10th Ave
8th Ave
6th Ave
Arguello Blvd
Art Museum
Golden Gate Park
U.C. Medic Cente

ABC-TV

Name: Maria Rossi
Based in: Sydney
Signature: Maria Rossi

ROSSI 559088 MC
Valid from 7/87 until end 92

Maria Rossi is a reporter for ABC-TV Sydney.

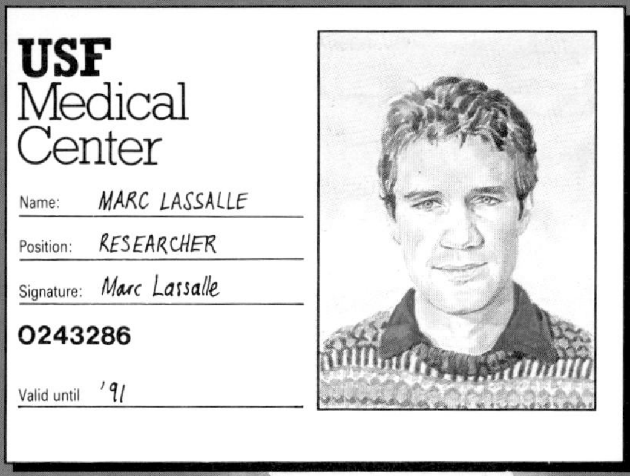

USF Medical Center

Name: MARC LASSALLE
Position: RESEARCHER
Signature: Marc Lassalle
0243286
Valid until '91

Marc Lassalle is a medical researcher from Canada. He is living in San Francisco now.

SEALS

Matt Jackson is a baseball player. He plays for the San Francisco Seals.

Fumiko and Felipe are studying English in the United States. They are staying with American host families.

Central San Francisco

Palace of Fine Arts/ Exploratorium
Yacht Harbor
Fisherman's Wharf
Fort Mason
Coit Tower
San Francisco Bay
The Embarcadero
Marina
Beach St
Baker St
Cervantes Blvd
Chestnut St
Lombard St
Russian Hill
Telegraph Hill
Columbus Ave
Mason St
Stockton St
Powell St
Hyde St
Polk St
Van Ness Ave
Franklin St
Gough St
Fillmore St
Divisadero St
Presidio Ave
Union St
Union Street
Pacific Heights
Broadway
Ferry Building
Jackson St
Transamerica Pyramid
Washington St
Chinatown
Nob Hill
Financial District
Sacramento St
California St
Japantown
Sutter St
Post St
Geary St
O'Farrell St
Geary Blvd
Union Square
San Francisco – Oakland Bay Bridge
Western Addition
Masonic Ave
Civic Center
Moscone Convention Center
1st St
2nd St
3rd St
4th St
5th St
6th St
7th St
8th St
9th St
10th St
Turk St
Golden Gate Ave
Fulton St
Hayes St
Mission St
Howard St
Folsom St
Harrison St
Bryant St
Univ. of San Francisco
Panhandle
Fell St
Oak St
Haight St
Market St
Cole St
Clayton St
Ashbury St
Roosevelt Way
14th St
Mission Dolores
Kansas St
17th St
Mission
3rd St
Twin Peaks
Portola Dr
Potrero
S.F. General Hospital
Castro St
Church St
Dolores St
Mission St
South Van Ness Ave
Potrero Ave
24th St
Clipper St
Army St

0 1 mile
0 1 km

1 Help!

MATT: Help! Help!
I'm down here!
MAN: Are you OK?
MATT: Yes, I am.
Later . . .
MAN: What's your name?
MATT: Matt Jackson.
MAN: What do you do?
MATT: I'm a baseball player.
MAN: Where do you live?
MATT: In San Francisco.

1

Look and listen. Answer *true* or *false*.

1 Matt Jackson is OK.
2 He is a baseball player.
3 He lives in San Diego.

Language focus

2

Ask and answer about you, like this:

> What's your name?
> . . . .

3

Look at the pictures and say the names.

Lisa:
doctor

Bud:
actor

Ken:
businessman

Carmen:
student

4

Ask and answer for *them*, like this:

> Lisa, where do you live?
> — In San Diego.

5

Look at the pictures and say the occupations. Ask and answer, like this:

> Bud, what do you do?
> — I'm an actor.

6

Ask and answer about you, like this:

What's your name?
— Satoko.
Where do you live?
— In Tokyo.
What do you do?
— I'm a teacher.

Interaction 1 **page 72**

Hi

Conversation practice

1

Look and listen.

2

Have similar conversations.

Read and write

3

Read this. Then copy and complete the form.

I am Diane Harper and I live in Oakland, California. I am a translator.

Name ....
Home ....
Occupation ....

Write about you in the same way.

I am .... *and I* ....
I am a(n) ....

Numbers

4

Say the following numbers:

0	1	2	3	4	5
zero/"oh"	one	two	three	four	five
6	**7**	**8**	**9**	**10**	
six	seven	eight	nine	ten	

5

Say the following telephone numbers:

a (415) 423–8765
b (619) 295–4386
c 935–7298
d 649–2386
e (213) 521–6257
f (808) 861–3518

Interaction 2 **page 72**

Listening and acting out

Grammar and usage

What's your name? (= What is)
— [Lisa].
Where do you live?
— In [San Diego].
What do you do?
— I'm a [doctor]. (= I am)

What's yours? How about you?

2 Missing

Two days earlier:

POLICEMAN: Good afternoon, ma'am.
MARCIE: Good afternoon, officer.
POLICEMAN: Are you Mrs. Jackson?
MARCIE: Yes, I am.
POLICEMAN: Is your husband at home?
MARCIE: No, he isn't.
POLICEMAN: Where is he?
MARCIE: I guess he's at the ball park.
POLICEMAN: No, Mrs. Jackson. He isn't at the ball park . . .

1

Look and listen. Answer *true* or *false*.

1 Mrs. Jackson is at home.
2 Mr. Jackson is at the ball park.
3 The policeman knows Mrs. Jackson.

Language focus

2

Look at the family tree and say the words.

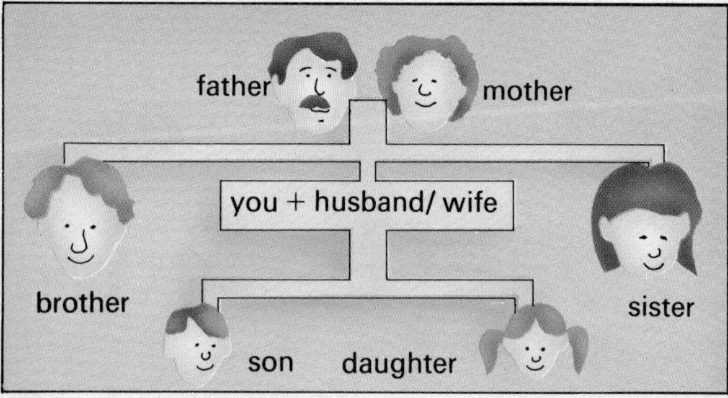

3

Now draw your own family tree.

4

Ask and answer about you, like this:

Is your father a businessman?
— Yes, he is. / No, he isn't.

Is your sister a teacher?
— No, she isn't.
What does she do?
— She's a doctor.

5

Look at the pictures and say the words.

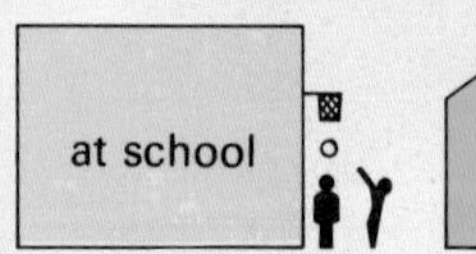

6

Ask and answer, like this:

Where's Ken?
— He's at work.

Interaction 1 **page 73**

She's at Jean's

2

Conversation practice

1 

Look and listen.

2

Have similar conversations.

Ask for	*he/she's at*	*number*
Andy	Jim's	666–2978
Lisa	work	712–6051
Ken	home	234–2499
Bud	Richard's	461–1500

Read and write

3

Read about Lisa and Ken and answer the questions.

Lisa Sherman is a doctor, and she lives in San Diego. She isn't at home right now. She's at work.

1 What does Lisa Sherman do?
2 Where does she live?
3 Where is she now?

Ken Harper is a businessman, and he lives in Oakland. He isn't at work right now. He's at home.

1 What does Ken Harper do?
2 Where does he live?
3 Where is he now?

4

Ask and answer about your family, like this:

What does your brother do?
— He's a pharmacist.
Where does he live?
— In Los Angeles.
Where is he now?
— At home, maybe.

5

Write about someone in your family.

My . . . . *is a(n)* . . . ., *and* . . . .
lives . . . . *He/she's* . . . .

Interaction 2 **page 73**

Listening and acting out

Grammar and usage

Is your [brother] a [pharmacist]?	
— Yes, he is./No, he isn't.	(= is not)
What does your [sister] do?	
— She's a [doctor].	(= She is)
Where does she live?	
— She lives in [Boston].	
Where's [Ken]?	(= Where is)
— He's at [work].	(= He is)
— He's at [Jim's].	(= Jim's home)

Hello. This is Felipe.	Please.
Do you have the number?	Thank you.

3 Marc asks for directions

Excuse me!

MARC: Excuse me!
MAN: Yes?
MARC: Where's the Golden Gate Gym?
MAN: The Golden Gate Gym? I'm sorry, I don't know.
MARC: Thanks anyway . . . Excuse me!
WOMAN: Yes?
MARC: Where's the Golden Gate Gym?
WOMAN: It's on Van Ness Avenue, across the street from the movie theater. Go down one block and turn right.
MARC: Thank you.
WOMAN: You're welcome.

1

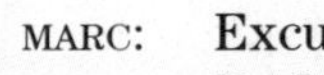

Look and listen. Which one is the Golden Gate Gym?

Language focus

2

Look at the picture of Union Avenue and say the words.

3

Ask and answer, like this:

Where's the bank?
— It's on Union Avenue, next to the grocery store.

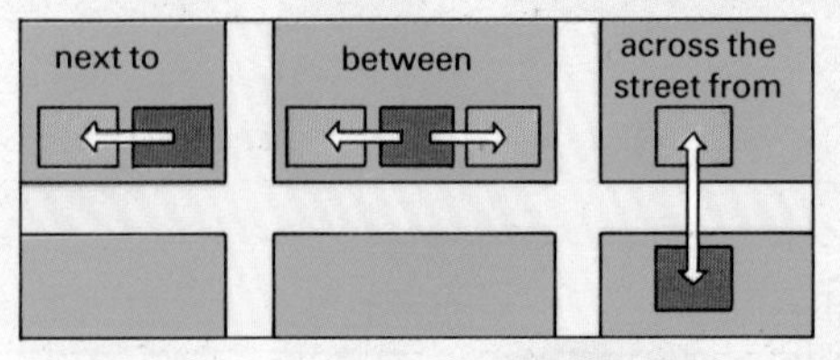

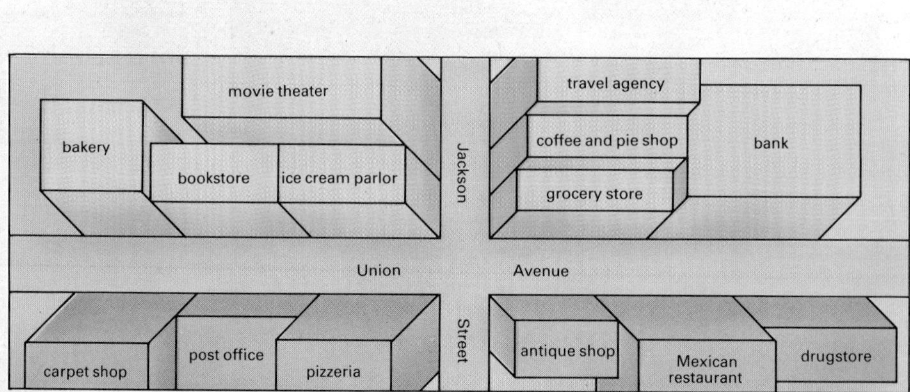

4

Have conversations like this:

Excuse me!
— Yes?
Where's the bookstore?
— It's on Union Avenue, between the bakery and the ice cream parlor.
Thank you.
— You're welcome.

Here you are

Conversation practice

1 

Look and listen.

2

Have similar conversations. Here are some words you can use:

knife pepper salt	tea coffee sugar	on	shelf table

Read and write

3

Read this.

Ken and Diane Harper live in Oakland, California, near San Francisco. Their house is on Western Avenue, next to the high school.

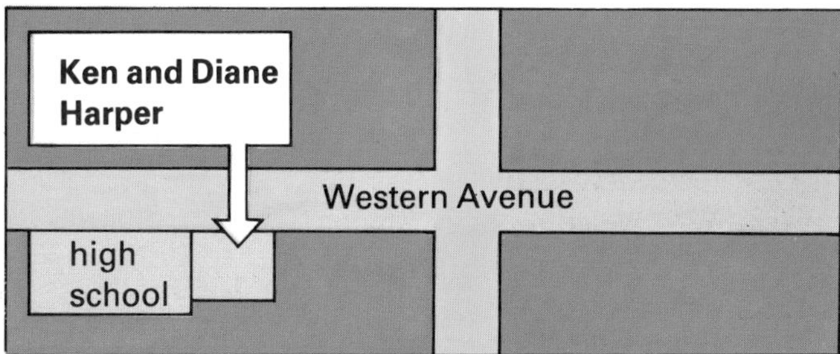

Oakland, near San Francisco

4

Write similar paragraphs about the following:

Del Mar, near San Diego

Toluca, near Mexico City

Interaction 1 **page 74**

Listening and acting out

Grammar and usage

Where's the bank?
— It's on [Union Avenue], (= It is)
[next to the grocery store].

Excuse me! Sure. You're welcome.
Can I have the [salt], please?
— Here you are.

4 At the Golden Gate Gym

PETER: Hello. I'm Peter Ling.
MARC: I'm Marc Lassalle.
PETER: I'm sorry. What's your name again?
MARC: Marc. Marc Lassalle.
PETER: Are you American?
MARC: No, I'm not.
PETER: Where are you from?
MARC: I'm from Canada. But I live in San Francisco now. I'm a medical researcher.
PETER: Well, welcome to the Golden Gate Gym, Marc! Now let me see . . . How old are you?
MARC: I'm twenty-five.
PETER: And where do you live?
MARC: 1502 Union Street.

1

Look and listen. Choose the correct answers from the chart.

Name:	Marc Lassalle
Nationality:	American/ Canadian
Home (now):	San Francisco/ Canada
Occupation:	medical researcher/ translator

Language focus

2

Look at the pictures. Repeat the names.

3

Ask and answer, like this:

Where's Pedro from?
— He's from Mexico. He's Mexican.

4

Ask and answer about you, like this:

Are you American?
— No, I'm not.
Where are you from?
— I'm from Spain. I'm Spanish.

Read and write

5

Read this. Write the information in a box, like the one below.

Miguel Garcia is a teacher. He's Spanish, and he lives in Madrid, Spain.

Name ______	*Home* ______
Occupation ______	*Nationality* ______

6

Now write a similar paragraph about a friend or member of your family.

Nice to meet you

Conversation practice

1 

Look and listen.

2

Have similar conversations. You can use the names of these people.

Carlos Mexico City *Mexican*	Alfio Rio de Janeiro *Brazilian*	Emilia Lisbon *Portuguese*
Seiji Kyoto *Japanese*	Tim and Sue Adelaide *Australian*	Richard Denver *American*

Numbers

3

Say the following numbers:

11	eleven	19	nineteen	80	eighty
12	twelve	20	twenty	90	ninety
13	thirteen	21	twenty-one	100	one hundred
14	fourteen	30	thirty	101	one hundred one
15	fifteen	40	forty		
16	sixteen	50	fifty	1,000	one thousand
17	seventeen	60	sixty	1,001	one thousand one
18	eighteen	70	seventy		

4

Ask and answer, like this:

How old is Carmen?
— She's twenty-one.

Carmen	Atsuko	Pedro	Karl	Luis	Sylvie
21	23	28	25	56	37

5

Ask and answer about you, like this:

How old are you?
— Twenty-eight./That's a secret!

Interaction 1 **page 75**
Interaction 2
Listening and acting out

Grammar and usage

Where's [Pedro] from?
— He's from [Mexico]. He's [Mexican].
Are you [American]?
— No, I'm not.

How old are you?
— I'm [twenty].
How old is [Carmen]?
— She's [twenty-one].

I'm [Pascale], and this is [Jean-Paul].
— Nice to meet you./Hi.

5 Just curious

MARC: Hi, Linda, how are you?
LINDA: Fine, thanks.
MARC: Say, where were you last night? You weren't here.
LINDA: No, I wasn't.
MARC: Were you at the movies?
LINDA: No, I wasn't.
MARC: Out to dinner?
LINDA: No . . .
MARC: Where were you, then?
LINDA: At the theater.
MARC: The theater? Were you alone?
LINDA: No.
MARC: Who were you with?
LINDA: My father!

1

Look and listen.
Which is the correct statement?

a Linda was at the movies last night.
b Linda was at the theater last night.
c Linda was at home last night.

Language focus

2

Say these words:

yesterday morning
yesterday afternoon
last night

3

Ask and answer about you, like this:

> Were you at home/school/work yesterday afternoon?
> — Yes, I was./No, I wasn't.

4

Say the days of the week:

Monday
Tuesday
Wednesday
Thursday
Friday
Saturday
Sunday

5

Ask and answer about you, like this:

Where were you on Monday morning?
— I was at work.
Where was your husband on Wednesday afternoon?
— He was at the travel agency.

Here are more words to help you.

the doctor's

the office

the shopping center

the bank

Interaction 1 **page 76**

Conversation practice

1

Look and listen.

2

Ask and answer, like this:

What time is it? — It's ten o'clock. — It's noon/midnight.

a  d  g  j 

b e 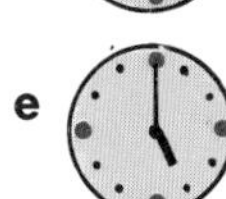 h 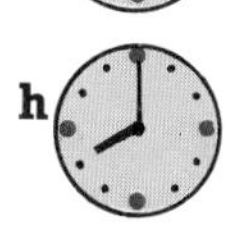 k

c f 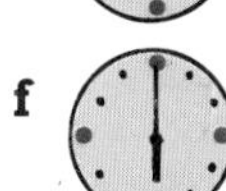 i  l 

3

Have similar conversations. Use this information.

cafe

ice cream parlor

restaurant

gym

theater

Read and write

4

Read this, then complete the chart below.

Seiji Ozawa is the conductor of the Boston Symphony Orchestra. He lives in Boston.

Yesterday morning he was in Washington, and yesterday afternoon he was in New York.

Last night he was back in Boston for a concert.

Name	Home
Occupation	
Where?	
Yesterday morning	
Yesterday afternoon	
Last night	

Write a similar paragraph about Chris Snyder.

Name *Chris Snyder*	Home *Del Mar*
Occupation *tour guide*	
Where?	
Yesterday morning	*Los Angeles*
Yesterday afternoon	*Sausalito*
Last night	*Los Angeles – show*

Interaction 2 **page 76**
Listening and acting out

Grammar and usage

Were you at [home] last night?
— Yes, I was./No, I wasn't. (= was not)
Where were you [yesterday afternoon]?
— I was at the [bank].

What time is it?
— It's [ten] o'clock.

This is [Fumiko]. I forgot! I'm sorry.

6 Departure

Whose camera equipment is this?

GROUND HOSTESS: Passengers for San Francisco, please come this way.
RALPH: Here we go, Maria!
MARIA: Today Sydney, tomorrow San Francisco.
SECURITY GUARD: Excuse me, everybody. Whose camera equipment is this?
RALPH: Oh, no! I forgot my camera! It's mine. Thank you.
SECURITY GUARD: Are you a cameraman?
RALPH: Yes, with ABC-TV Sydney.
SECURITY GUARD: Oh! Is that jacket yours, too?
RALPH: Oh, no. That's hers. . . . Maria! Your jacket.
MARIA: Oh, thanks!
SECURITY GUARD: That's all right.

1

Look and listen. Answer the questions with *yes* or *no*.

1 Is Ralph a TV reporter?
2 Is the camera equipment Ralph's?
3 Is the jacket Maria's?
4 Are Ralph and Maria in San Francisco?

Language focus

2

Look at the pictures and say the words.

3

Ask and answer:

Whose sweater is this/that? —It's Carmen's.
Whose shoes are these/those? —They're Miguel's.

4

Look:

mine	ours
yours	yours
his	theirs
hers	

The sunglasses

Conversation practice

1

Look and listen.

2

Now have similar conversations.
You can ask about the following things:

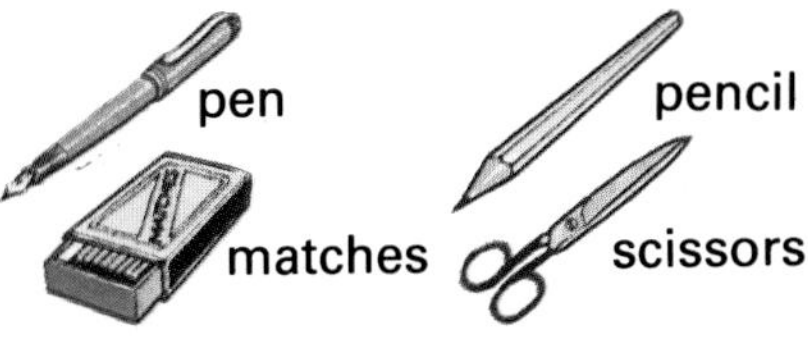

lighter
gloves

Read and write

3

Read this information, then answer the questions.

Bud is an actor. He lives in Sydney, but he isn't Australian. He's American, and he's from Denver. Bud's wife is Canadian. Her name is Joan. Bud's in-laws (Joan's family) live in Toronto.

1 What does Bud do?
2 Where does he live?
3 Where's he from?
4 Where is Bud's wife from?
5 Where do Bud's in-laws live?

4

In pairs, ask and answer questions about Lisa Sherman. Then write a similar paragraph.

Name:	Lisa Sherman
Occupation:	Doctor
Present home:	San Diego
Nationality:	British (from Manchester)
Husband's name:	Greg.
Husband's nationality:	American
Home of husband's family:	Los Angeles

Interaction 1 **page 77**
Interaction 2
Listening and acting out

Grammar and usage

Whose [sweater] is this?/ Whose [book] is that?
— It's [Danny's].
Whose [shoes] are these?/ Whose [gloves] are those?
— They're [Lori's]. (= They are)

It's mine/yours/his/hers.

I guess they're [Julie's]. Are these yours?
Can I borrow them?

7 A mistake

CLERK: Good morning, ma'am. Can I help you?
MARIA: Yes, please. Do you have *Time* magazine?
CLERK: No, ma'am. We don't have any . . .
MARIA: Well, then, do you have *The San Francisco Chronicle*?
CLERK: No, we don't. This isn't . . .
MARIA: You don't have any newspapers or magazines? This *is* a bookstore, isn't it?
CLERK: Yes, it is. But we don't sell newspapers, and we don't have any magazines. You can try the drugstore across the street.
MARIA: The drugstore?!!

1 

Look and listen. Answer *true* or *false*.

1 She has *Time* magazine.
2 Maria wants a book.
3 Drugstores sell newspapers.

Language focus

2

Look at the pictures. Match the words with the numbers.

3

Ask and answer, like this:

> Does the woman have a camera in her bag?
> — No, she doesn't.
> Does the man have any cigarettes in his briefcase?
> — Yes, he does.

4

Ask and answer about you, like this:

What do you have in your pockets?
— I have my keys and a pen.

Do you have any books in your bag?
— No, I don't.

a camera
b tickets
c keys
d cigarettes
e lighter
f pen
g gloves
h passport
i book
j postcards

Would you like a cookie?

Would you like a cookie?

Sure, thanks.

Gee, we don't have any cookies, but we have some donuts. Would you like one?

Thanks, Julie.

Conversation practice

1

Look and listen.

2

Look:

We don't have *any* cookies, but we have *some* donuts.

3

Have similar conversations, like this:

Would you like ....?
Sure, thanks.
Gee, we don't have any ...., but we have some .... Would you like one?
Thanks, ...

Here are some words you can use:

Interaction 1 **page 78**
Interaction 2
Listening and acting out

Grammar and usage

Does [the woman] have any [keys]?
— Yes, she does./No, she doesn't. (= does not)

We don't have any cookies, but we have some donuts.

Would you like a donut?
— Sure, thanks.

8 The next big game

MARIA: This is Maria Rossi for ABC-TV Sydney. I'm here at Fletcher Field, home of the famous San Francisco Seals. Their manager, Ron Bellugi, is with me now. Hi, Ron.

RON: Hi, Maria.

MARIA: Ron, your last big game was on September 27th, and the next one is on Thursday night. Who's the pitcher for the big game?

RON: Matt Jackson.

MARIA: Is he here now?

RON: No, he isn't.

MARIA: Oh? Where is he?

RON: That's the problem. I don't know!

1 

Look and listen. Answer the questions.

1 When was the last big game?
2 When is the next game?
3 Who is the Seals' pitcher?

Language focus

2

Say the names of the months:

January	July
February	August
March	September
April	October
May	November
June	December

3

Say the following numbers:

1st first	**9th** ninth	**17th** seventeenth
2nd second	**10th** tenth	**18th** eighteenth
3rd third	**11th** eleventh	**19th** nineteenth
4th fourth	**12th** twelfth	**20th** twentieth
5th fifth	**13th** thirteenth	**21st** twenty-first
6th sixth	**14th** fourteenth	**22nd** twenty-second
7th seventh	**15th** fifteenth	**30th** thirtieth
8th eighth	**16th** sixteenth	

4

Say the following dates:

a January 1st
b October 3rd
c November 4th
d March 27th
e July 5th
f May 12th
g April 30th
h February 2nd

5

Ask and answer about you, like this:

When's your birthday?
— October 31st. When's yours?

The time

Language focus

1

Study the big clock.

2

Ask and answer, like this:

> What time is it?
> — **(g)** It's a quarter to five.

a
b
c
d
e
f
g
h

five to
five after
ten to
ten after
a quarter to
a quarter after
twenty to
twenty after
twenty-five to
twenty-five after
(*six*) thirty

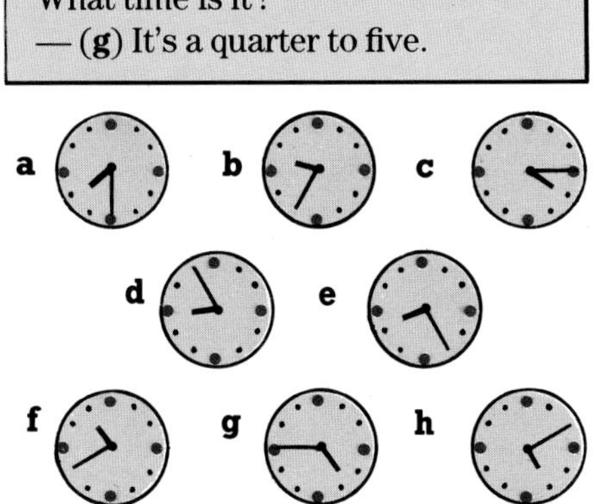

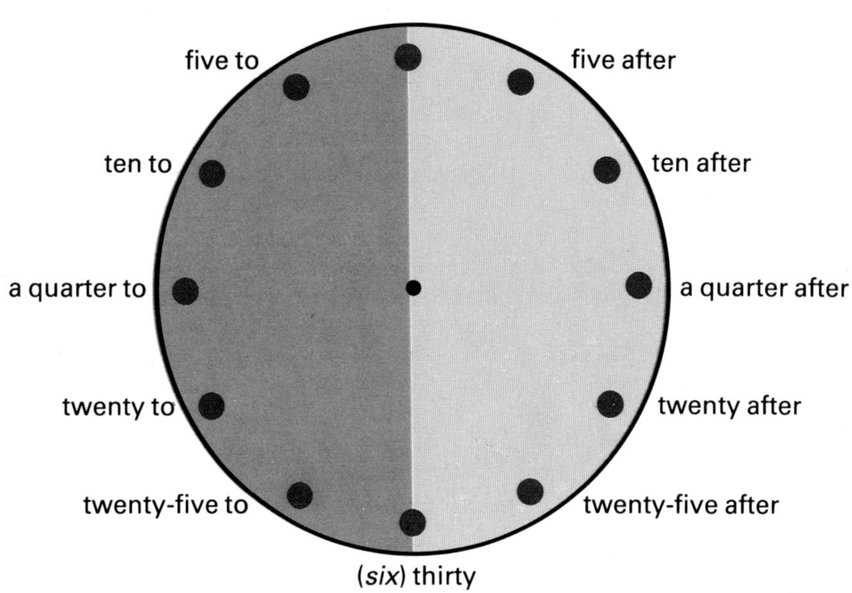

Read and write

3

Read this text about Ken Harper. Write the information from it in a chart like the one below.

4

Write more sentences about Ken. Use the information in the chart on the right.

Ken Harper was in Oakland on Sunday, August 23rd. He was at home with his wife, his son, and their dog, Spot.

On Monday, August 24th, he was in Los Angeles with two clients. On Monday evening, they were at the Music Center. The Music Center is downtown, near City Hall.

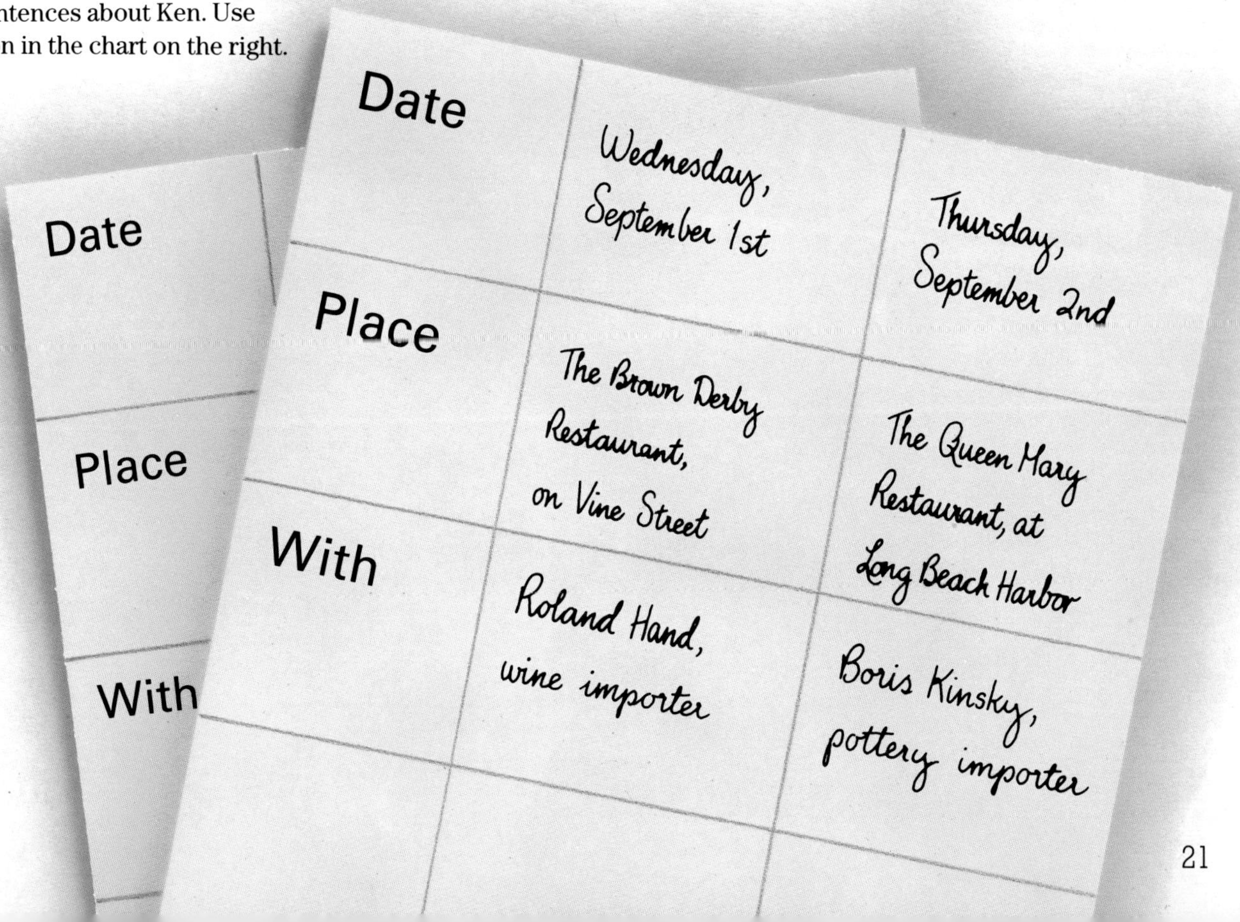

Date
Place
With
Date
Wednesday, September 1st
Thursday, September 2nd
Place
The Brown Derby Restaurant, on Vine Street
The Queen Mary Restaurant, at Long Beach Harbor
With
Roland Hand, wine importer
Boris Kinsky, pottery importer

8 A hotel room

Conversation practice

1

Look and listen.

2

Have similar conversations, like this:

.... May I help you?
Yes. I'd like to ....
Certainly. For when?
....
Yes, that's fine. May I have your name, please?

Here are some words you can use:

A.C.T. Theater	reserve two seats	March 1st
Giorgio's Restaurant	reserve a table for two	10 o'clock tonight
Sassoon's Hairstylists	make an appointment	Thursday morning at 11 o'clock
Budget Rent-a-Car	rent a car	November 1st, for the weekend

Review

3

You meet Felipe for the first time at a party.

FELIPE: Excuse me!
YOU: ....?
FELIPE: What time is it, please?
YOU: ....
FELIPE: Thanks.
YOU: ....?
FELIPE: Felipe.
YOU: ....
FELIPE: Nice to meet you. Where are you from?
YOU: ....
FELIPE: Oh really? I'm from Brazil. I'm a lawyer. What do you do?
YOU: ....
FELIPE: I see. Where do you live?
YOU: ....

Reading

1

Read the following questions. Answer them with *yes* or *no* by reading the text.

1 Is Ken Harper a pilot for Ace Airways?
2 Was Ken Harper happy with his flight to Bombay?
3 Does Ken travel to Africa on Ace?

ACE AIRWAYS

Ken Harper is a regular passenger on **ACE AIRWAYS**. This is what he says about **ACE**:

"Two years ago I went to Bombay on another airline. The service was poor, and the plane was six hours late! I read about Ace in *Time*. Now I travel to Canada, Europe and the Orient on **ACE**. I like using **ACE** for business trips!"

ACE AIRWAYS flies all over the world. Daily flights to Europe, South America and the Orient; weekly flights to Africa. Fly **ACE**. Tomorrow's airline today.

Interaction 1

Work in pairs. Put the conversation in the correct order. Write *first, second, third,* etc. above the sentences.*

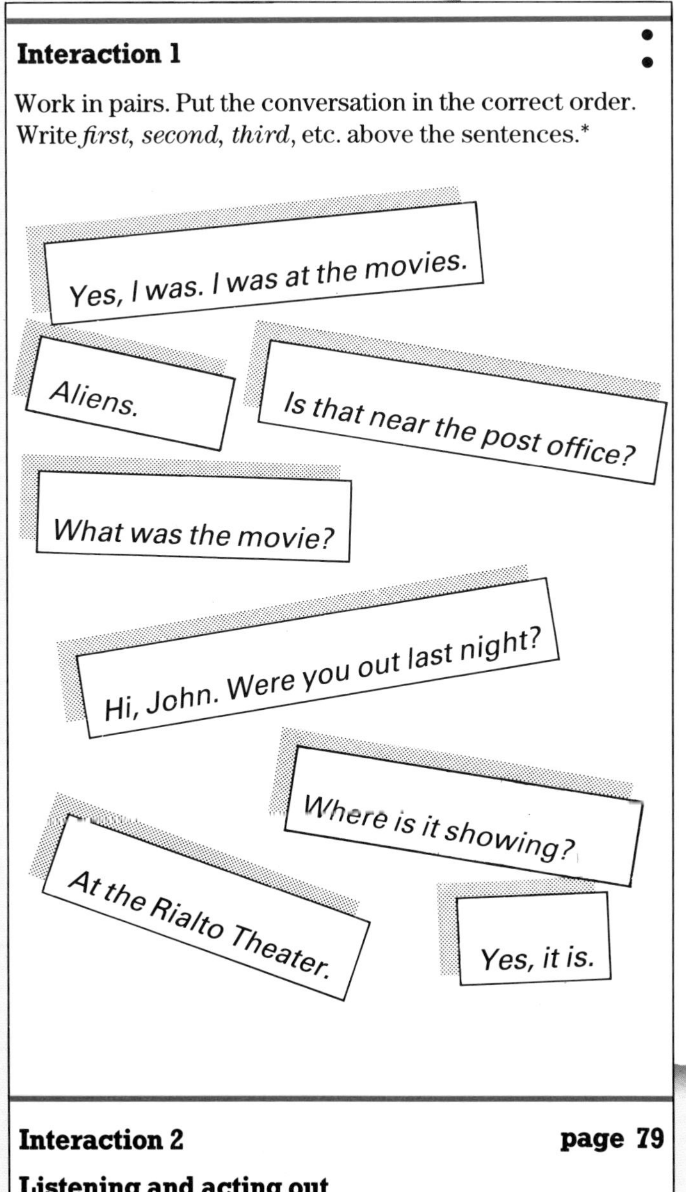

Interaction 2 **page 79**

Listening and acting out

* see Teacher's Manual for alternative presentation.

Grammar and usage

When's your birthday? (= When is)
— [July 5th].

What time is it?
— It's [a quarter] to/after [six].
— It's [two thirty].

I'd like to reserve a room, please.
— Certainly. That's fine.

9 What do people in San Francisco eat?

MARIA: Excuse me! Do you have a minute?
MARC: Uh . . . I guess so.
MARIA: I'm from ABC-TV Sydney. Can I ask you some questions?
MARC: OK.
MARIA: Good . . . thanks. Do you like tacos?
MARC: Yes, I do.
MARIA: How about spaghetti?
MARC: Spaghetti! Yes . . . yes, I do.
MARIA: And paella?
MARC: I don't know. I've never tried it.
MARIA: How about sashimi?
MARC: Raw fish? No . . . yuck! Look, I have to go.
MARIA: Wait, wait. How about steak?
MARC: I love steak. But I hate surveys! Oh, there's my bus. Bye!

1

Look and listen. Complete the chart about Marc with *yes*, *no* or *?* (I don't know).

Language focus

2

Look at the pictures and repeat the words.

3

Ask and answer about you, like this:

Do you like steak?
— Yes, I do./No, I don't.
Do you like sashimi?
— I don't know. I've never tried it.

4

Ask and answer about food from your country.

Read and write

5

Read this:

Marc Lassalle likes tacos, spaghetti and steak, but he doesn't like sashimi. He has never tried paella.

Now write a similar paragraph about a classmate.

Food

Language focus

1

Match the pictures with the words.

2

Look at the pictures below. Ask and answer, like this:

> What's Spaghetti Bolognese?
> — It's an Italian dish with ground beef, tomatoes, and onions.

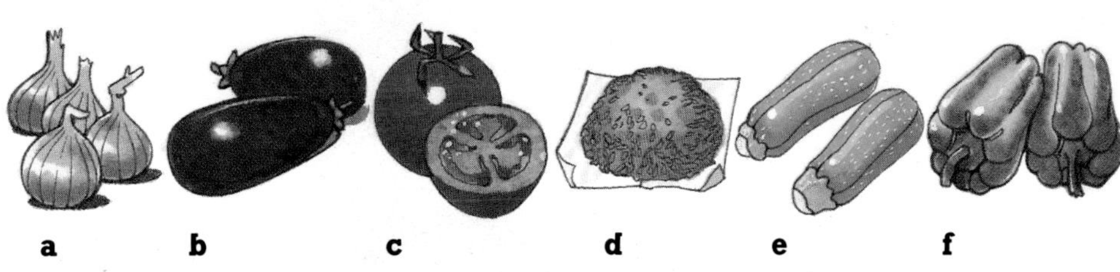

1 ground beef **2** onions **3** tomatoes

4 eggplant **5** zucchini **6** peppers

Chiles Rellenos
Mexican

peppers
ground beef
onions
cheese

Spaghetti Bolognese
Italian

spaghetti
ground beef
tomatoes
onions

Ratatouille
French

eggplant
zucchini
tomatoes
onions

Read and write

3

Read this. Then make questions and answer them. Use the words below.

1 Do people all over the world/ hamburgers?
2 Does a hamburger/ham in it?
3 Where/name hamburger come from?
4 /hamburgers easy to cook?

People and food: the hamburger

People all over the world like the "all American" hamburger. But why "*ham*burger"? It doesn't have any ham in it! The name hamburger actually comes from Hamburg, Germany. In the nineteenth century many Germans emigrated to the United States. They sailed from Hamburg. Hamburgers were easy to cook for the passengers. So the hamburger emigrated too!

Conversation practice

1

Look and listen.

2

Have similar conversations, like this:

What's your favorite kind of music /exercise?	What's your favorite sport /pastime?
I like .... best.	
I like .... too.	I don't. I like ....

Here are some words you can use.

Review

3

Match the sentences. Then put them in the right order.

Paul	*John*
1 I like it. When's our next class?	**a** At 10:30.
2 See you then.	**b** Sure. Go ahead.
3 Is this your lighter?	**c** It's OK. How about you?
4 Thanks. Would you like a cigarette?	**d** Yes, it is.
5 Were you at the last class?	**e** Bye.
6 What time?	**f** Tuesday.
7 No, I wasn't here. Do you like English?	**g** No, thanks.
8 Can I borrow it?	**h** Yes, I was. Weren't you?

Reading

1

Read the following questions. Then answer them by reading the text.

1 Where were Marc and his friends on Saturday evening?
2 Does Marc like San Francisco?

2

Match the times with the pictures.

1 Saturday evening
2 Saturday morning
3 4 P.M. on a weekday
4 Friday evening

a

b

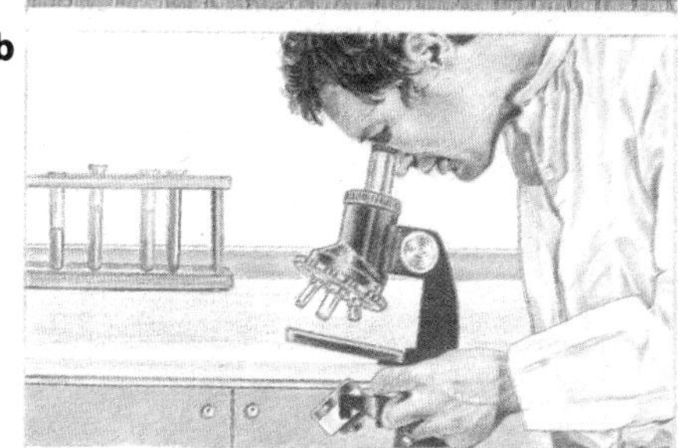

c

d

Interaction 1 **page 80**

Listening and acting out

Grammar and usage

Do you like [Chiles Rellenos]?
— Yes, I do. / No, I don't. (= do not)
— I don't know. I've never tried it. (= I have)
What's [Spaghetti Bolognese]?
— It's [an Italian dish] with [ground beef], [tomatoes], and [onions].

What's your favorite kind of [music]?
— I like [classical music] best.
I like [classical music] too. / I don't.

10 A daily routine

Maria Rossi interviews Hawaiian sumo wrestler Takanofuji at the Japantown Fall Festival.

MARIA: Good morning, Mr. Takanofuji.
TAKANOFUJI: Good morning.
MARIA: May I ask you some questions?
TAKANOFUJI: Certainly.
MARIA: When do you work out?
TAKANOFUJI: Hmmph! Every day, of course.
MARIA: Oh, sorry . . . uh . . . when do you usually get up?
TAKANOFUJI: At five o'clock.
MARIA: How do you get to work?
TAKANOFUJI: By car.
MARIA: Oh! And what do you usually have for lunch?
TAKANOFUJI: Chicken, beef, fish and vegetables, and a pound of rice.
MARIA: Really! That's a lot of food.

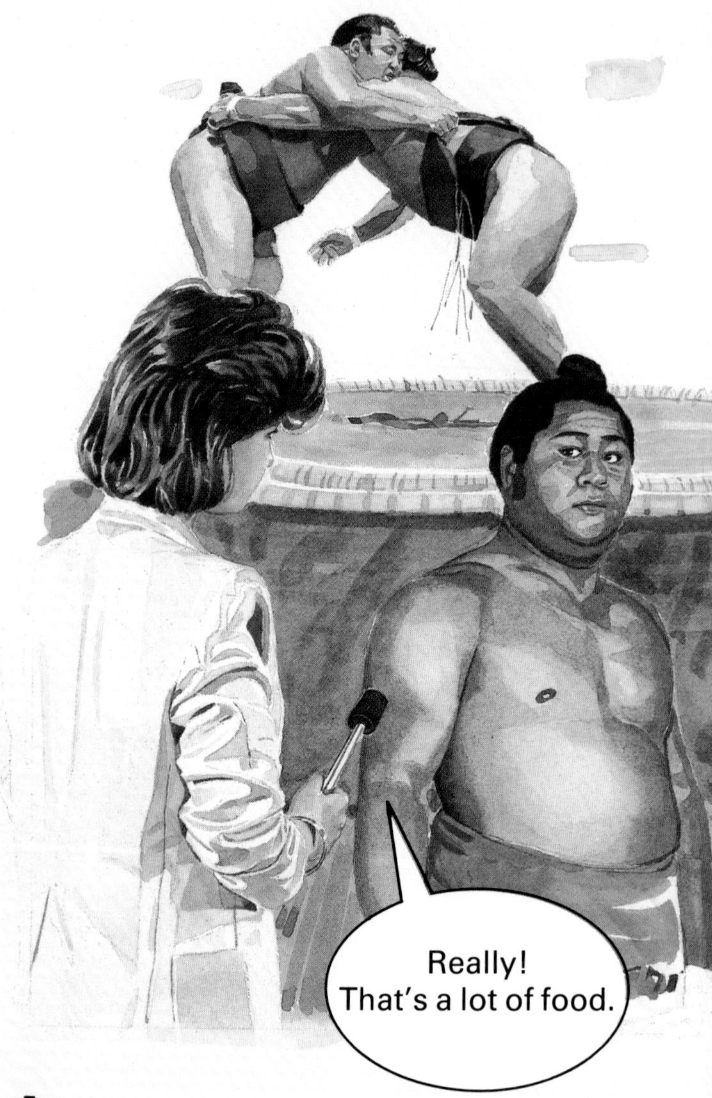

1

Look and listen. Answer *true* or *false*.

1 He works out every day.
2 He gets up at five o'clock.
3 He gets to work by bike.
4 He has a light lunch.

Language focus

2

Look at the pictures and say the words.

get up

have breakfast

leave home

get to work/school

get home

go to bed

3

Ask and answer about you, like this:

What time do you get up?
— At seven thirty.

4

Look at the pictures and say the words.

5

Ask and answer about you, like this:

How do you get to work?
— By train.

Language focus

1

Say these expressions:

on weekends

on Mondays

in the evening

2

Now look at the pictures and say the words. Ask and answer about you, like this:

> What do you do in the evening?
> — I usually listen to music.

At home	Going Out	Exercise/Sport
entertain friends	go to a restaurant	play soccer
listen to music	go to the movies	go jogging
read	go for a drive	go swimming

Read and write

3

Read the text about Ken. Then make questions and answer them, like this:

What / Ken /do?
What does Ken do?
— He's a businessman.

1 Where/ live?
2 Where/work?
3 What /wife's/name?
4 When /get up?
5 What / have for breakfast?
6 When /get home?
7 What /in the evening?

Ken Harper is a businessman. He is 37. He works in downtown San Francisco at the Hi-Tech Corporation headquarters on the thirty-fourth floor of the Transamerica building.

He and his wife, Diane, usually get up at seven o'clock in the morning. Ken has toast, an egg, yoghurt and coffee for breakfast. Then he takes "BART" (the subway) to work. He usually gets home from work at seven o'clock in the evening. Then he watches the news on TV. Ken and Diane usually entertain friends on weekends.

4

Look at the pictures and write a similar story about Carmen Gonzalez.

10 A bus to Chinatown

Conversation practice

1

Look and listen.

2

Have similar conversations. Use the map and information below, or your local bus or subway map.

Which bus goes to ....?
Take the number ..... and transfer at .... to the { number ..... / .... cable car line.
How much is it?
....
How often do they come?
About every .... minutes.

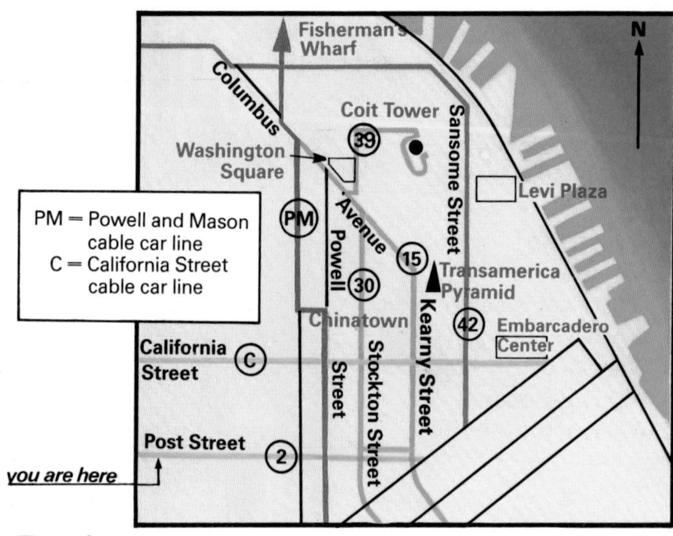

Review

3

You are talking with Julie.

YOU: ....?
JULIE: I like Italian food best.
YOU: ....?
JULIE: Indian food? I don't know. I've never tried it.
YOU: ....?
JULIE: Well, I usually eat at the Italian restaurant on Union Street in North Beach.
YOU: ....?
JULIE: Near Washington Square.
YOU: ....?
JULIE: It usually opens at 11 o'clock.

Reading

1

Read the following questions. Then answer them by reading the text.

1 Who were the first jeans for?
2 Why were they popular in the 1850s?
3 Are all jeans cheap today?

Levi Strauss made the first blue jeans in the 1850s for the California gold miners. Jeans (or Levis) were cheap and durable, so the miners liked them. But by the 1960s young people everywhere were in jeans. A new gold rush? No, they were popular again because they were still cheap and durable and *not* part of the world of high fashion. They were not part of the world of social class and competition.

Today the world is different. Jeans are different too. They can be expensive and very fashionable. Famous movie stars wear them, and so do princesses. What would Levi Strauss think of that?

Gold prospecting in California in 1849

Interaction 1

Find someone who:

a plays a musical instrument ....
b gets up at 6:30 A.M. ....
c reads a newspaper during/after breakfast ....
d was out for a drive in the country last weekend ....
e goes jogging ....
f eats at a restaurant after class ....
g likes horseback riding ....
h lives near you ....
i can sing your favorite song ....

Interaction 2 **page 81**

Listening and acting out

Grammar and usage

What time do you [get home]?
— At [a quarter to seven].
How do you get to [work]?
— By [bus].
What do you do [on weekends]?
— I usually [play tennis].

Which bus goes to [Chinatown]?
How much is it?

11 Lost!

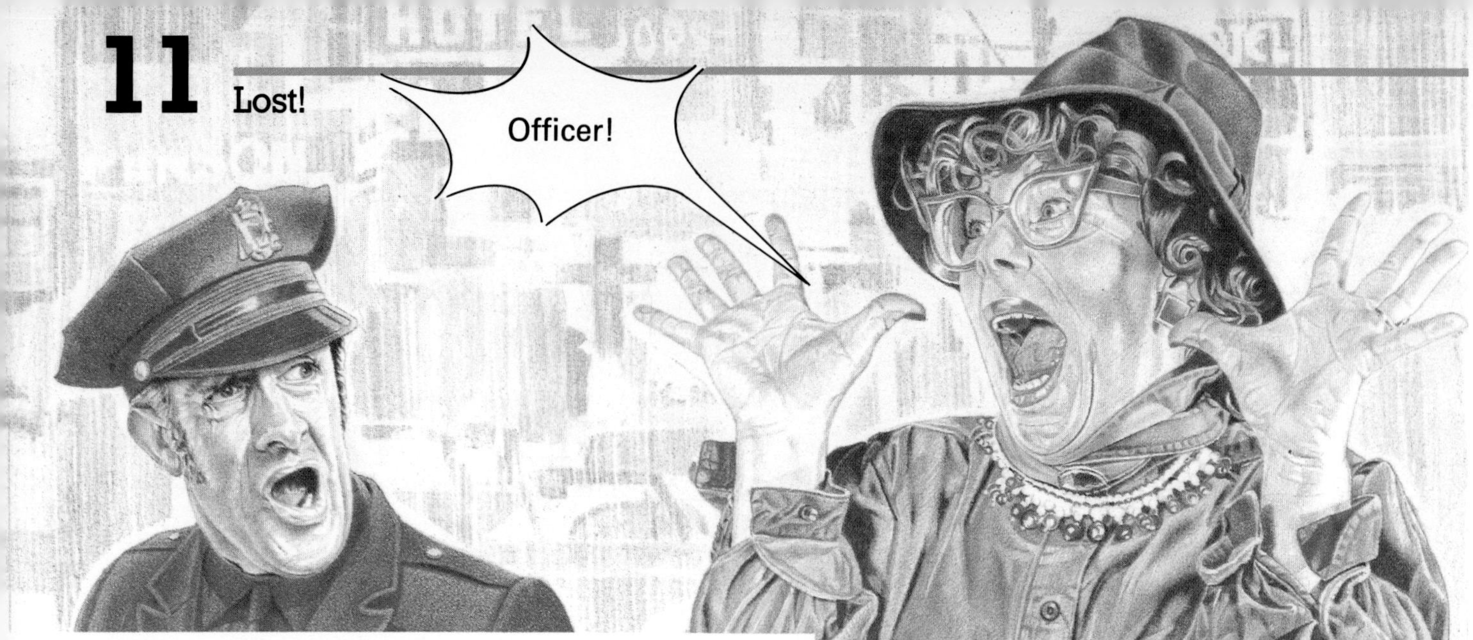

CAROL: Officer! Officer!
POLICEMAN: Yes, ma'am. What's the problem?
CAROL: It's Dennis. He's lost!
POLICEMAN: Oh, I see. What does he look like?
CAROL: He's young and good-looking with white hair and blue eyes . . . and black spots.
POLICEMAN: Black spots? Is your son sick?
CAROL: Dennis isn't my son, officer.
POLICEMAN: Oh? Who is he, then?
CAROL: He's my dog!

1

Look and listen. Which one is Dennis — **a**, **b**, **c**, or **d**?

a **b** **c** **d**

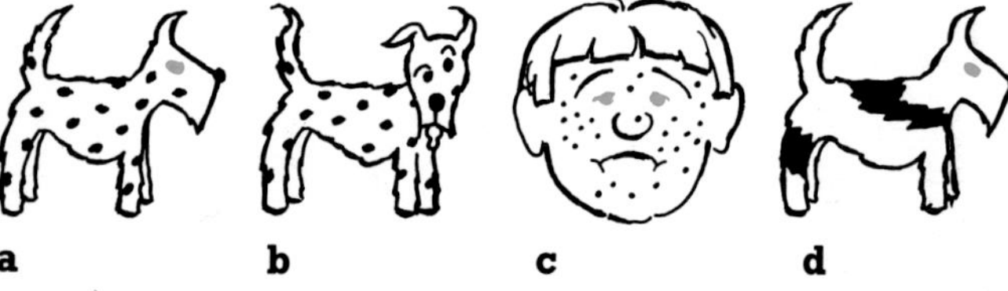

Language focus

2

Look at the pictures and say the words.

blue eyes | brown eyes | green eyes

brown hair | black hair | gray hair | white hair | blond hair | red hair

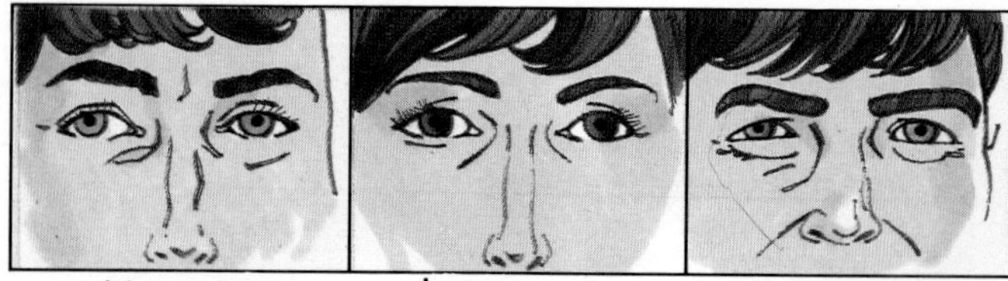

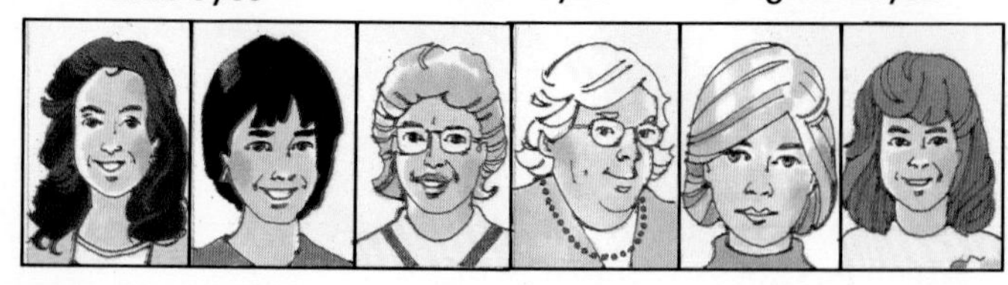

3

Ask and answer, like this:

> What color is Pedro's hair?
> — It's black.
> What color are Sylvie's eyes?
> — They're blue.

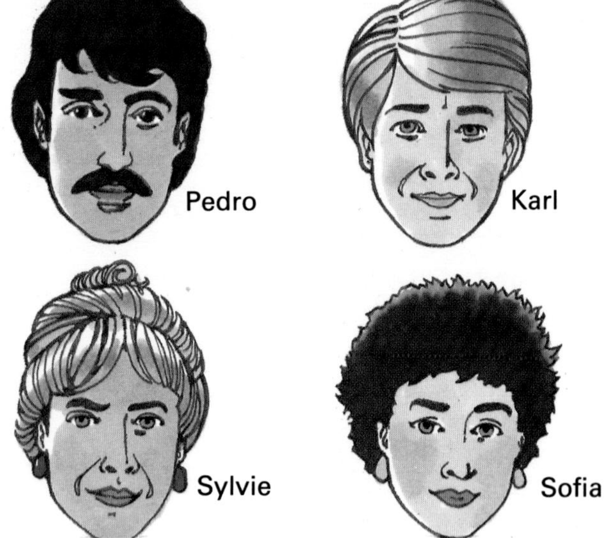

4

Ask and answer about your family, like this:

> What color is your mother's hair?
> — It's gray.

11

What does she look like?

Language focus

1

Look at the pictures and say the words.

2

Look at the Harper family. Ask and answer, like this:

> What does Ken's mother look like?
> — She's short with gray hair.

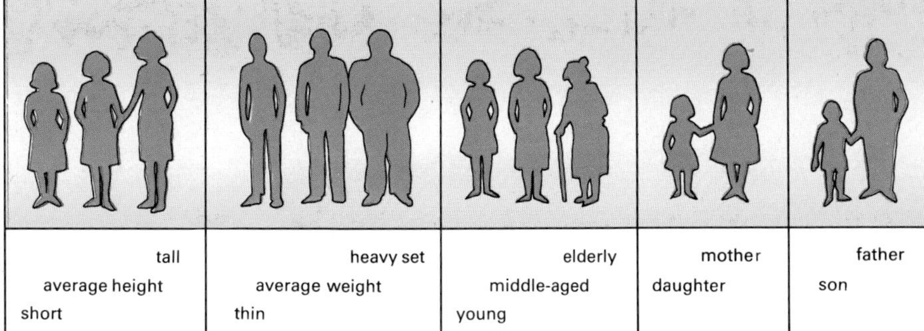

3

Ask and answer about your family, like this:

> What does your brother look like?
> — He's thin with brown eyes and brown hair.

Ken Harper | Ken's mother, Grace | Ken's son, Andy | Ken's wife, Diane

Read and write

4

Look at the picture on the right, then read the text.

Laura Dyson is thirty-four years old. She is short with brown eyes and blond hair. She is a computer programmer from England, but she lives in the United States.

Now write a similar paragraph about her husband, Malcolm (33/ businessman / Scotland).

Interaction 1 **page 82**

11 A new sweater

Conversation practice

1

Look and listen.

2

Have similar conversations, like this:

Can I help you?
Yes, please. I'd like ....
Certainly. Which color?
............, please.
What size?
.........., I guess.
Here you are.
Thanks.

Here are some words you can use:

one of	these those	sweaters	shirts	ties
a pair of	these those	pants	shoes	earrings

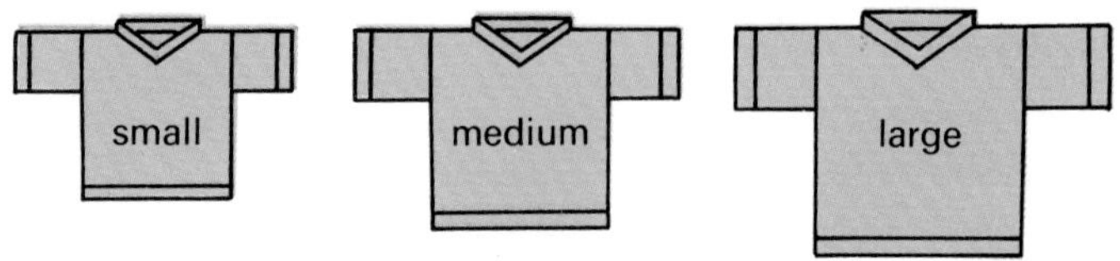

Review

3

You are talking with Fumiko.

FUMIKO: Where were you last night?
YOU: ....
FUMIKO: Was it a good movie?
YOU: ....
FUMIKO: What do you usually do in the evening?
YOU: ....
FUMIKO: I usually watch television. Do you like TV?
YOU: ....
FUMIKO: I like the nature programs best. How about you?
YOU: ....

Reading

1

Read the following questions. Then answer them by reading the text.

1 Who watches or plays baseball every year?
2 Find out the following information about Yankee Stadium:
  a the number of games every year.
  b the number of hot dogs consumed at a game.
  c the number of employees.

BASEBALL

Take Me Out to the Ball Game!

Do you like baseball? Can you play the game? Every year millions of Americans, Canadians, Latin Americans and Japanese watch and play baseball. It is one of the most popular games in the U.S.A. with 26 teams in the two major leagues and thousands of amateur teams.

Yankee Stadium in New York has 81 games every year and 2,400,000 spectators. At a typical game, 30,000 spectators consume 20,000 hot dogs, 30,000 cans of beer and 45,000 cans of Coca-Cola. You can understand why Yankee Stadium has 600 employees!

The Yankees in action

Interaction 2

1 Make two teams.
2 Write a different word from Unit 11 (e.g. tall, young) in each space below.
3 A member of team A chooses a number from 1–16.
4 A member of team B says his or her word for that number.
5 The member of team A uses that word in a question or sentence. If it's correct, team A gets one point.

Note: Choose a number only once.

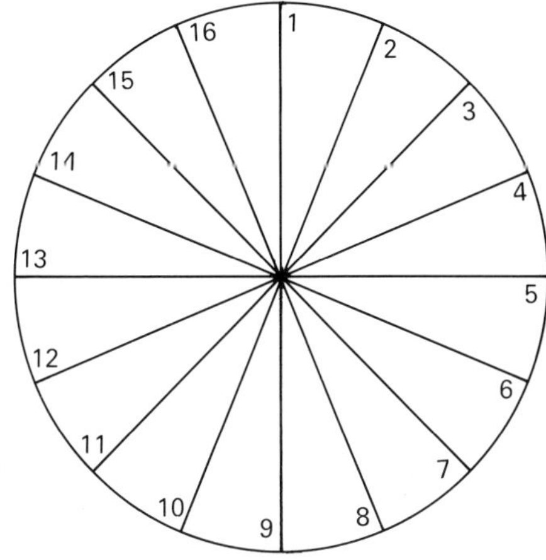

Listening and acting out page 82

Grammar and usage

What color are [Sylvie's] eyes?
— They're [blue].
What does [Diane] look like?
— She's [tall] with [blond hair].

Can I help you? Which color? What size?

One	of those	sweaters.
A pair	of these	shoes.

12 Marc and Maria meet again

Are these seats free?

RALPH: Excuse me. Are these seats free?
MARC: Yes, sure. Go ahead.
RALPH: Thanks.
MARIA: Oh, hi! It's you again.
MARC: Oh, hello. Do you live around here?
RALPH: No. We're from Sydney, Australia.
MARIA: Actually, I was born in Italy, but my family moved to Australia when I was three.
MARC: Can you speak Italian?
MARIA: Sure. How about you?
MARC: No, but I can speak French and a little Spanish.
RALPH: Are you American?
MARC: No, I'm Canadian, from Montreal. But I work here. I'm a medical researcher. What do you two do?
MARIA: I'm a TV reporter, and Ralph's a cameraman.
MARC: That sounds interesting.
MARIA: Yes, it is . . . usually.

1 

Look and listen. Answer *true* or *false*.

1 Ralph is from Australia.
2 Maria was born in Sydney.
3 Marc can speak French.

Language focus

2

Study the chart.

3

Ask and answer, like this:

Can Lisa cook?
— No, she can't.
Can Antonio cook?
— Yes, he can.

4

Ask and answer about you, like this:

Can you speak Portuguese?
— Yes, I can. / No, I can't.

	drive	type	cook	play the piano	speak Portuguese
Lisa	yes	yes	no	yes	no
Antonio	yes	no	yes	no	yes

12 Around the city

Language focus

1

Look at the tourist information and say the names.

2

Ask and answer, like this:

> Where can I take a bay cruise?
> — You can try the Red and White Fleet on Pier 41.

Ask about:

1 a good seafood dinner (*eat*)
2 a good view of San Francisco (*get*)
3 a good exhibition (*see*)
4 some souvenirs (*buy*)
5 a nice hat (*buy*)
6 a good country and western band (*hear*)

FISHERMAN'S WHARF
Dozens of fine seafood restaurants.

The Asian Art Museum
in Golden Gate Park.
10 A.M. to 5 P.M.

Twin Peaks
Finest view of the city!

The Bay Company
at Fisherman's Wharf.
Gifts, souvenirs and film.
Open from 9 A.M. to 10:30 P.M.

The Mad Hatter
at Fisherman's Wharf.
Hats for everyone!

Bay cruises
The Red and White Fleet on Pier 41. For cruise information, call 546–2810.

Paul's Saloon
Scott Street
Best country and western music (Thursday, Friday, Saturday nights).

Read and write

3

Read this, then copy and complete the chart.

Peter Savage likes hiking, fishing and good restaurants. He can hike and fish all day, but he can't go into town for dinner. He goes fishing at 5 o'clock every morning with his dog, Fang.

Name
Likes
Can
Can't
Activities

4

Write a similar paragraph about Bud Stevens, the actor.

Name *Bud Stevens*
Likes *Spicy food, fast cars, music*
Can *cook, play the guitar*
Can't *read music*
Activities *jogging with wife Joan every morning*

Say, Hans, you look worried!

I am. I can't do this homework!

Do you want some help?

Yes, thanks.

Conversation practice

1

Look and listen.

2

Now match the sentences below. For example:

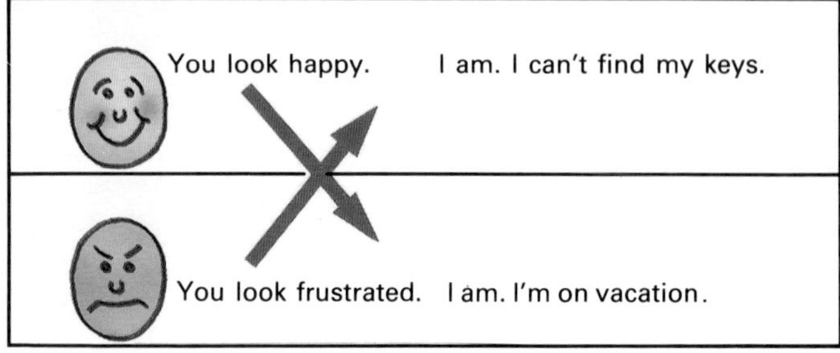

1 You look tired.	**a** I am. I have nothing to do.
2 You look pleased.	**b** I am. I can't start my car.
3 You look bored.	**c** I am. I can't open the window.
4 You look frustrated.	**d** I am. I forgot my sweater.
5 You look busy.	**e** I am. I have a new job.
6 You look cold.	**f** I am. I was on the train for three hours.
7 You look hot.	**g** I am. I have a lot to do.

3

Now look at possible suggestions and replies and complete the conversations. For example:

> You look tired.
> — I am. I was on the train for three hours.
> Do you want to take a nap?
> — No, that's all right.

Suggestions	*Replies*
Do you want to go to a movie?	That's a good idea.
Do you want some help?	Yes, thanks.
Do you want to borrow one?	No, that's all right.
Do you want to take a nap?	

4

Now practice the conversations.

Reading

1

Read the following questions. Then answer them by reading the text.

1 Was Matt Jackson at work yesterday?
2 Does he usually get to the ball park early or late?
3 Was he at home yesterday afternoon?

Jackson Missing

Foul Play Suspected

The Press Syndicate
San Francisco, CA — Matt Jackson, the top pitcher for the San Francisco Seals, is missing and nobody can find him. "We are worried," Ronald Bellugi, the Seals' manager, said. "Matt always comes to the ball park early, and he never leaves before seven thirty. Yesterday we were all at the ball park, as usual, waiting for Matt. But he didn't show up." His wife, Marcie, is also worried. The police are questioning a neighbor. She saw three men get into a car yesterday morning. One of them was Matt Jackson, she believes.

Interaction 1

1 Make a chart like this:

Activity	Student	Can do	Likes to do
1 Skiing	Marie	yes	yes
2			
3			

2 Think of ten things people do when they are not at work: for example, skiing, cleaning the house, cooking. Use your dictionary or ask your teacher for help.

3 Write the ten things in the chart.

4 Ask five other students in the class
 a what things on the chart they can do.
 b what things on the chart they like to do.

5 Tell the class what you found out.

Interaction 2 **page 83**

Listening and acting out

Grammar and usage

Can [Antonio] play the piano?
— Yes, he can./No, he can't. (= cannot)
Where can I [see] a good [exhibition]?
— You can try the [Asian Art Museum].

You look [worried].
Do you want some help?
— No, that's all right. (= that is)

13 An argument

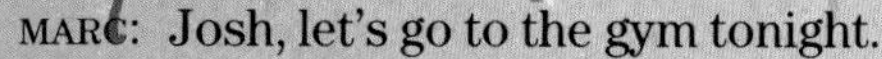

MARC: Josh, let's go to the gym tonight.
JOSH: No, thanks. I want to watch TV. Carol's cooking program is on.
MARC: But you always watch TV!
JOSH: That's not true! Sometimes I listen to music.
MARC: All right. But you never go out, and you never exercise! Every evening you sit and do nothing! You just watch TV.
JOSH: What's wrong? Don't you like American TV?
MARC: No, I don't.
JOSH: Well, I do!
MARC: All right. You watch TV! I'm going to the gym.

1

Look and listen. Answer *yes* or *no*.

1 Does Josh watch TV every night?
2 Does Josh go out every night?
3 Does Josh exercise?
4 Does Marc like American TV?

Language focus

2

Look at the diagram and say the words.

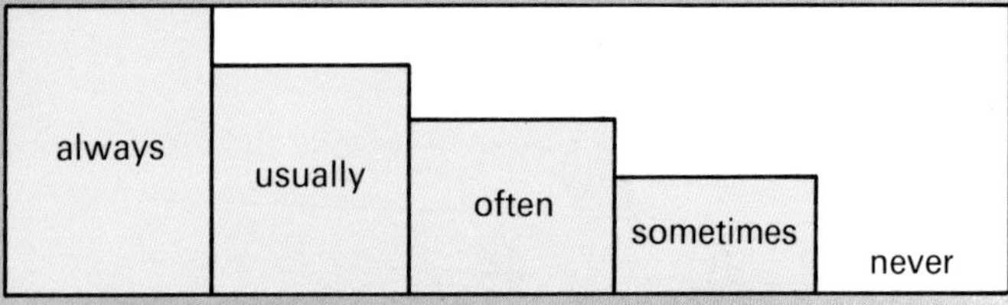

Look at the two brothers and study the chart.

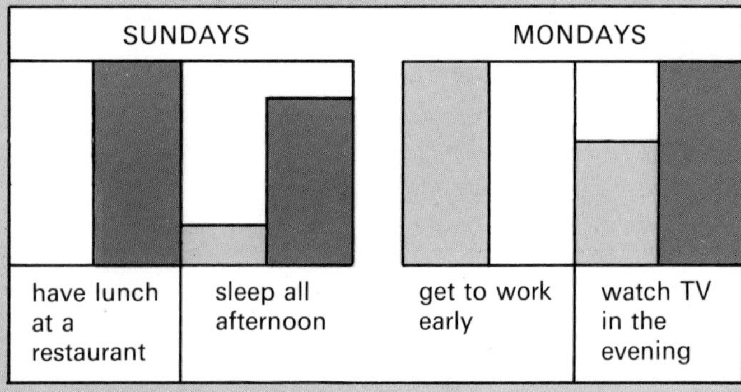

3

Ask and answer, like this:

> What does Simon do on Sundays?
> — He always has lunch at a restaurant.
> — He usually sleeps all afternoon.

4

Ask and answer about you, like this:

What do you do on Saturdays?
— I always read the newspaper in the morning, and I usually go jogging in the afternoon.

Language focus

1

Look at the diagram and say the words.

2

Ask and answer about you, like this:

> Do you have a hobby?
> — Yes, I play the guitar.
> How often do you play?
> — About twice a week.

Mon	Tues	Wed	Thurs	Fri	Sat	Sun	
	●						once (a week)
				●		●	twice (a week)
		●	●	●			three times (a week)
●		●	●			●	four times (a week)
●	●		●	●		●	five times (a week)
	●	●	●	●	●	●	six times (a week)
							never

Read and write

3

Read this letter and answer the questions.

1. What does Carol do?
2. When does she get up in the mornings?
3. What does she do on weekends?

4

Write a similar letter to an American friend about you. Say what you do every day and on weekends.

Dear Nicole,

You say you want to know about the life of a TV personality! Well, it's not easy. How can I begin?

I usually get up at 5:30 and put on my make-up. Then I walk my dog, Dennis. I always have breakfast with George, my husband, and Dennis.

Then I go to the studio. My fans are usually at the front door, so I always go in the back door. I love them, but I never have time in the morning.

We record the show from 9 to 11. Then we have a big lunch. I go home at 6 pm. In the evening, I usually watch old movies on my video.

On weekends, George and I often go out to dinner or entertain friends at home. The life of a TV host is a lot of fun. Don't forget to try my new recipe book!

Sincerely,
Carol

13 The guitar

Conversation practice

1

Look and listen.

2

Have similar conversations, like this:

Say, Pascale, do you ....?		
Yes.		
Do you .... very well?		
No, not very well.	Oh, not too badly.	Yes, pretty well.
Would you .... me ....?		
Sure.	Maybe some other time.	

Here are some words to help you:

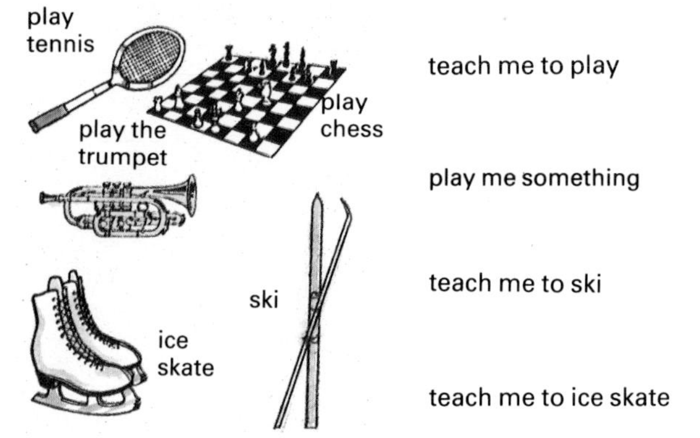

Review

3

You are talking with Fumiko.

FUMIKO: You look tired.
YOU: ....
FUMIKO: Oh. Whose party was it?
YOU: ....
FUMIKO: What time was the party over?
YOU: ....
FUMIKO: Really! When do you usually go to bed?
YOU: ....
FUMIKO: It's no wonder you're tired! Would you like a cup of coffee?
YOU: ....

Reading
1

Read the following questions. Then answer them by reading the text.

1 How is San Francisco like Sydney?

2 What can you do for fun in San Francisco?

Maybe you're sitting on your patio and barbecuing some steaks. Maybe you're thinking about Sydney's sister city — San Francisco. Like Sydney, San Francisco is a city on a bay, and it has an international atmosphere. It has over 4,200 restaurants from many countries, and a large immigrant population. A third of all San Franciscans come from bilingual homes. San Francisco has a Chinatown, a Japantown and a Hispanic area — the "Mission."

San Francisco is a good place for young people. You can see movies from the U.S., Europe, Latin America and Japan. You can listen to music in a concert hall or under the stars. You can go to the theater, go dancing or just sit and watch the boats from the Marina on a Sunday afternoon. That's what I'm doing right now!

— Maria Rossi, reporting for ABC-TV from San Francisco.

Interaction 1 **page 84**
Interaction 2
Listening and acting out

Grammar and usage

What does [Simon] do on [Mondays]?
— He [always] [watches TV in the evenings].
How often do you [play]?
— About [three times] a week.

Do you play very well?
— Oh, not too badly.
Would you [play] me [a song]?
— Sure.

14 Cooking with Carol

CAROL: Hello again, everybody. Welcome to "Cooking with Carol." Today's recipe is Mexican omelette. Dennis and my husband, George, love my omelettes. Anyway, here's the omelette. It's frying in the pan. Now I'm putting in all the extra ingredients . . . onion, tomato, potato and peppers. Mmm . . . wonderful! It smells delicious! Let's wait a minute and . . . yes, it's ready. Now I'm putting the omelette on this plate and — oops! Oh, no! Now I'm picking the omelette off the floor. I guess this one's for George.

1

Look and listen. Put the pictures in the correct order.

a

b

c

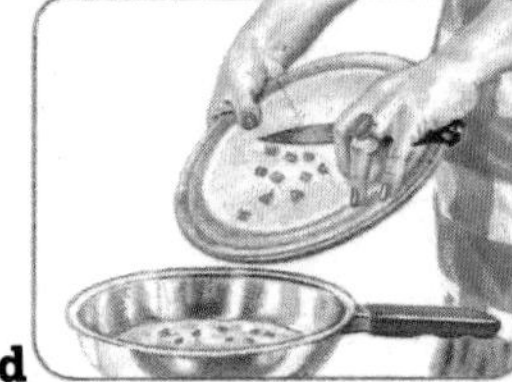
d

Language focus

2

Match the descriptions with the pictures and people on the right.

chopping an onion
washing the dishes
making coffee
tasting a sauce
peeling potatoes
frying an egg

3

Ask and answer, like this:

> What's Sofia doing?
> — She's tasting a sauce.
> What are Chris and Sharon doing?
> — They're peeling potatoes.

4

Ask and answer about you, like this:

What's your sister doing right now?
— I guess she's having lunch.

On vacation

Language focus

1

Match these words with the pictures:

camping   driving   climbing   sailing

2

Ask and answer, like this:

> What does Lisa do?
> — She's a doctor.
> Is she visiting a patient right now?
> — No, she isn't. She's sailing in the Caribbean.

Lisa — *doctor*

Sharon — *writer*

Bud — *actor*
Joan — *teacher*

Carmen and Miguel — *students*

Read and write

3

Read Joan's card to her mother. Then answer the questions:

1 What is Joan doing?
2 What is Bud doing?
3 Where do they usually stay?
4 What is Puebla like?

4

Write your own vacation postcard.

Hi Mom!
I'm lying in the sun having a nice, tall, cool drink. Bud is swimming in the pool. He has a good tan.
We drive every two days and we usually stay at inexpensive hotels. Mexico is beautiful and Puebla is a fascinating town with lots of interesting churches.
Love,
Joan and Bud

Mrs. G. Johnson
67 Summerhill Avenue
Toronto
Ontario
Canada M4T 1A9

Puebla: La Catedral, The Cathedral.

14 Coffee

Conversation practice

1

Look and listen.

2

Have similar conversations, like this:

I'm making .... Would you like a cup/ a glass/one?
Sounds good.
How do you like it/them?
.........., please.

3

Here are some words you can use:

hamburgers	with ketchup mustard onions cheese lettuce tomatoes	plain
coffee	with cream milk sugar	black
tea	with lemon sugar honey	plain
iced tea	with lemon sugar	plain

Review

4

You are talking with Fumiko.

YOU: ....?
FUMIKO: Hi. I'm fine, thanks.
YOU: ....?
FUMIKO: I'm looking at this skiing magazine.
YOU: ....?
FUMIKO: Yes, I can.
YOU: ....?
FUMIKO: Once a year, at least. I usually go on New Year's.
YOU: ....?
FUMIKO: Uh, not too badly, I guess. But my sister's a fantastic skier.
YOU: ....
FUMIKO: She's twenty-five.
YOU: ....?
FUMIKO: Sayako.

Reading

1

Put the pictures in the correct order by reading the text.

a

b

c

d

MARLOWE DETECTIVE AGENCY

File: X 15382 Brooks stakeout

Transcript of call by: Mike Leary

I think we have something. I'm calling from a café across the street from Buzz Brooks's illegal gambling house. Today, the city's big gamblers are betting on the Seals' game. Without Jackson in the game, the Seals are sure to lose. There's a guard standing at the door. Now a man with a baseball cap is coming out. I can't see his face. He's getting into a car. Now he's driving off. I'm following him. I'll get back to you!

2

Now answer the following questions.

1 Where is Detective Leary calling from?
2 What are the gamblers betting on?
3 Who is Detective Leary following?

Interaction 1

One student mimes an action. The others have to guess what it is. The student who guesses correctly gets a point. At the end of the game, the student with the most points wins.

Interaction 2 page 85

Listening and acting out

Grammar and usage

What's [Pedro] doing? (= What is)
— He's [frying an egg].
Are they [studying] right now?
— No, they aren't. They're [climbing in the Alps]. (= are not)

I'm making coffee.
How do you like it?
— With cream, please. / Black, please.

15 At the winery

MARIA: Ah, it's nice and cool in here.
GUIDE: This is our storage room for the Sebastiani Vineyards. We're getting ready for the harvest next month.
MARIA: How many of these large tanks are there?
GUIDE: Oh, about twenty.
MARIA: How much wine can they hold?
GUIDE: Around 8,000 gallons, ma'am.
MARIA: My goodness! There's a lot of wine in there! How many bottles is that?
GUIDE: About 40,000.
RALPH: That's enough for me for a lifetime!
GUIDE: With friends or alone?

How much wine can they hold?

1

Look and listen. Answer the questions.

1 When is the harvest?
2 How many large tanks are there?
3 How much wine can each tank hold?

Language focus

2

Study the map and say the words.

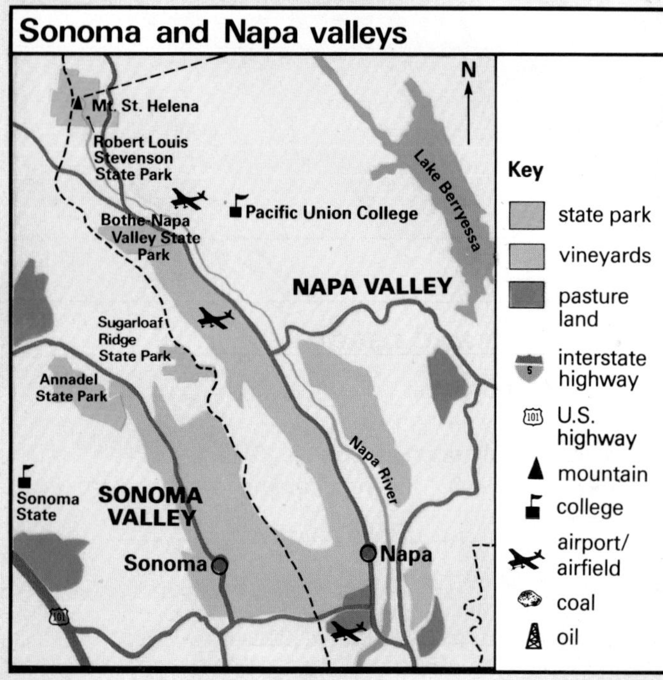

3

Ask and answer, like this:

Are there any lakes in Napa Valley?
— Yes, there's one.
Are there any airports in Sonoma Valley?
— No, there aren't.
Is there any oil in Sonoma Valley?
— No, there isn't.
Is there any pasture land in Napa Valley?
— Yes, there is.

4

Ask and answer about your region or country, like this:

Is there any oil in your country?
— Yes, there's a lot.
Are there any mountains?
— Yes, there are.

How much is there?

Language focus

1

Look at the pictures and say the words.

2

Ask and answer, like this:

> How many mushrooms are there?
> — There are a lot.
> How much meat is there?
> — There isn't any.
> How many tomatoes are there?
> — There aren't many.
> How much salt is there?
> — There isn't much.

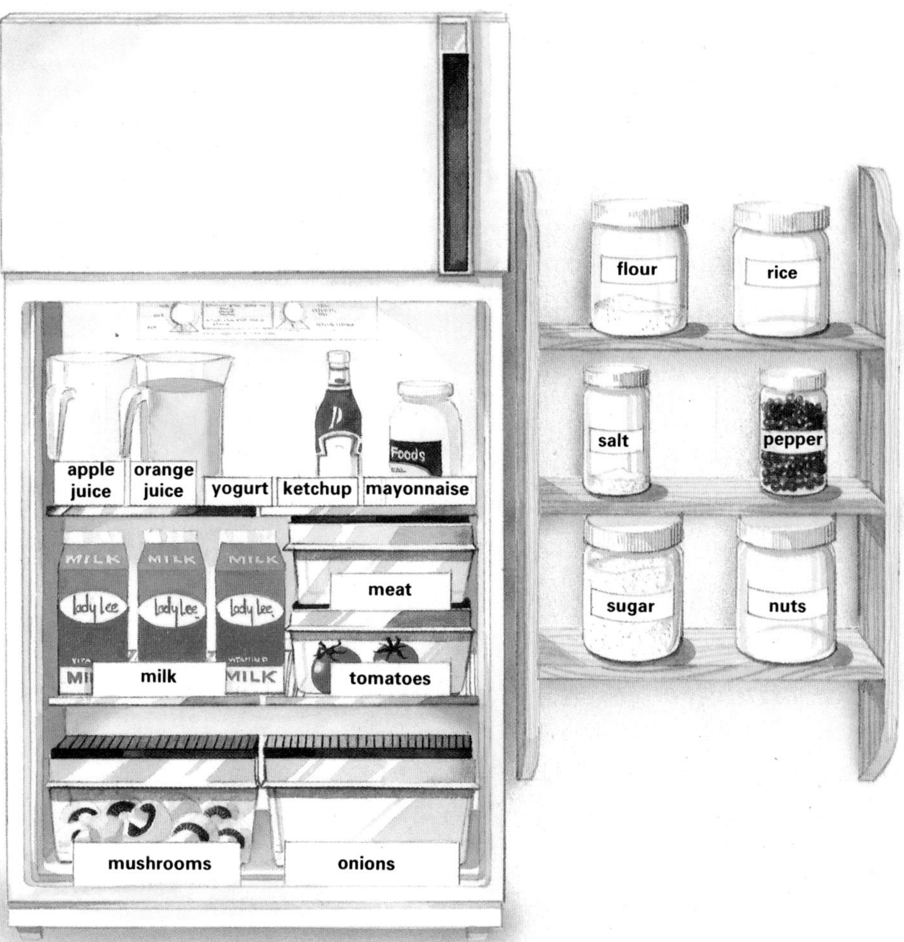

Read and write

3

Read the questions. Then answer them by reading the text.

1. How many acres of orchards are there today?
2. How much suburban development was there in 1930?
3. What was Santa Clara County like in 1930?
4. What is it like today?

4

Now write a similar paragraph about transportation in Los Angeles County. Here is some information.

1930	Today
public transport by rail (1,200 miles of railroad)	public transport by rail (6 miles of subway line)
0 freeways	19 freeways
0 smog	smog

From prunes to silicon

In 1930, there was a lot of agriculture in Santa Clara county. There were 100,000 acres of fruit orchards. There weren't any multinational firms, and there wasn't any suburban development.

Today, there isn't much agriculture, but there are a lot of multinational firms. There are only 10,000 acres of fruit orchards, but there are 40 big electronics companies. And there is a lot of suburban development.

The plum harvest in Santa Clara County

"Silicon Valley"

15 A flight to Paris

Conversation practice

1

Look and listen.

2

Have similar conversations. You can use the following information.

ACE AIRWAYS flights from San Francisco			
DESTINATION	DEPARTURES	ONE-WAY	ROUND-TRIP
Paris	Tu W F Sa Sun(2)	$1008	$2016
Honolulu	M Tu W Th Sa(3) Sun(2)	$ 386	$ 772
Montreal	Tu Th F Sa(2)	$ 295	$ 590
Tokyo	M Tu F Sun	$ 799	$1598
Singapore	Tu F	$1126	$2252
London	M Tu Th Sa(2) Sun	$1113	$2252
Caracas	Tu Th F Sa	$ 762	$1524
Sao Paolo	M Th	$1131	$2252

Note these expressions:

by | check
   | traveler's check
   | credit card

in cash

Review

3

You are talking with Pascale.

YOU: . . . .
PASCALE: Hello!
YOU: . . . . ?
PASCALE: I'm cleaning my violin.
YOU: . . . . ?
PASCALE: Not too badly.
YOU: . . . . ?
PASCALE: Play you a song? Maybe later.
YOU: . . . . ?
PASCALE: Coffee? No thanks, I have some tea. Would you like some?
YOU: . . . . ?
PASCALE: OK, I'll get it.

Reading

1

Read the following questions. Then answer them by reading the text.

1. Who found Matt Jackson?
2. Where is Matt Jackson now?
3. Does he have major cuts and bruises?
4. Where is Ron Bellugi going?

Missing Pitcher Found

Jackson Rescued By Man With Dog

The Press Syndicate

Ft. Bragg, CA — Matt Jackson is a lucky man. Yesterday Paul Shubin, a retired lawyer, found the Seals' pitcher along the rocky Mendocino coast.

Mr. Shubin and his dog Yipps

"I was out with my dog, Yipps. Suddenly Yipps started to bark. I was surprised. Yipps never barks. I looked down the cliff and there was Jackson."

Shubin rescued him with a rope from his camper. Then he drove him to Fort Bragg Hospital. Jackson has only minor cuts and bruises, but he is suffering from exhaustion.

Police say two men forced him into a car in San Francisco three days ago. But they are not giving out any other details. Ron Bellugi, the Seals' manager, was contacted immediately. "We are very happy Matt is safe," he said. "Maybe we can win the next big game with the Green Sox. Of course, we are waiting for the doctor's report. I'm flying up to Fort Bragg in twenty minutes."

Interaction 1 **page 86**
Listening and acting out

Grammar and usage

Are there any [lakes] in [Napa Valley]?
— Yes, there are. / No, there aren't.
Is there any [oil] in [Sonoma Valley]?
— Yes, there is. / No, there isn't.

How many [mushrooms] are there?
— There { are a lot. / aren't many/any.
How much [milk] is there?
— There { 's a lot. / isn't much/any.

How much is it round-trip? Let me see . . .
Are you paying in cash or by credit card?

16 Weekend plans

INSTRUCTOR: OK. That's all for tonight. See you next week.

MARC: Whew! That sure was hard work. I'm never going to be in shape.

FRIEND: Relax. You're not trying out for the Olympics. Anyway, what are you doing over the weekend?

MARC: I'm going to see that new play at the One Act Theater tomorrow night.

FRIEND: Who are you going with?

MARC: Maria.

FRIEND: Who's Maria?

MARC: She's a TV reporter from Australia. On Sunday we're going to have brunch together. Then we're going to hike up Mount Tam.

FRIEND: Sounds great.

1

Look and listen. Answer the questions.

1 What are Marc's plans for Saturday?
2 What are his plans for Sunday?

Language focus

2

Match Carmen's activities with the pictures.

get married
visit Italy
graduate
buy an apartment

July

September

August

October

3

Ask and answer, like this:

What's Carmen going to do in October?
— She's going to buy an apartment.

4

Ask and answer about you, like this:

What are you going to do next weekend?
— I'm going to see a movie on Saturday, and I'm going to visit my parents on Sunday.

16

Vacation plans

Language focus

1

Look at the pictures and say the words.

2

Match these activities with the pictures.

cook dinner	walk in space
play tennis	exercise
ride a motorcycle	go skiing

3

Ask and answer, like this:

> Why is Bud wearing shorts?
> — Because he's going to play tennis.

Read and write

4

Read this. Then copy and complete the information for Tour Number 1.

Next week Luis and his wife are going on vacation. First they are going to fly to London. Then they are going to travel around the south of England. During the week they are going to sail along the coast to Southampton, visit the Beaulieu Motor Museum and walk in the New Forest. This is their first trip to Europe.

5

Write about Karl and Ursula *or* Ken and Diane and the vacation they are going to take. Use the information in the advertisements. Karl and Ursula like sun and archaeology. Ken and Diane like good food and paintings.

Global Vacations: **Tour Number 1**

- ______ the south of England
- ______ the coast to Southampton
- ______ the Beaulieu Motor Museum
- ______ in the New Forest

Global Vacations: **Tour Number 2**

- spend a week in Paris
- fly to Charles de Gaulle airport
- stay in a luxury hotel
- climb the Eiffel Tower
- eat French food
- look at paintings in the Louvre

Global Vacations: **Tour Number 3**

- visit the land of the Maya
- fly to Guatemala City
- climb pyramids
- travel through Guatemala and Mexico
- swim in the Caribbean
- eat exotic food

16 A request

Conversation practice

1

Look and listen.

2

Have similar conversations, like this:

Are you going to take a walk?
No, I'm going to ....
Are you going to pass by the ....?
Yes, why?
Would you buy me ....?
Sure.

Here are some words you can use.

get a pizza	bakery	bread
get a newspaper	supermarket	milk
meet Fumiko for coffee	post office	stamps
go to the bank	deli	chicken sandwich

Review

3

You are talking with Jean-Paul.

JEAN-PAUL: Where do you live?
YOU: ....
JEAN-PAUL: How do you get to class?
YOU: ....
JEAN-PAUL: What do you usually do on weekends?
YOU: ....
JEAN-PAUL: What are you going to do next weekend?
YOU: ....
JEAN-PAUL: Well, I'm going to have a party on Sunday afternoon. Can you come?
YOU: ....?
JEAN-PAUL: At 3 o'clock.
YOU: ....?
JEAN-PAUL: Sure you can bring a friend. What's his name?
YOU: ....
JEAN-PAUL: What does he do?
YOU: ....
JEAN-PAUL: OK. See you Sunday. Bye!
YOU: Bye!

Reading

1

Read the following questions. Then answer them by reading the text.

1 What is the key to success, according to Iacocca?

2 How does Iacocca usually spend his weekends?

3 What does he do on Sunday nights?

4 Do all executives plan for vacations?

IACOCCA

Chrysler Chairman Lee Iacocca remarks on success:

"The ability to concentrate and use your time well is the key to success. I work hard during the week and, except for very difficult times, keep my weekends for my family and recreation. On Sunday nights I make a list of things to do in the coming week. I can't believe so many people can't control their schedules! When an executive says proudly, 'Boy, I worked so hard last year that I didn't take any vacation,' I want to say, 'You dummy! You can plan an $80,000,000 project, but you can't plan for taking a two-week vacation!'"

Interaction 1

Fill in the calendar below with your partner's activities for next week. Ask what he/she is going to do.

MONDAY	morning afternoon night
TUESDAY	morning afternoon night
WEDNESDAY	morning afternoon night
THURSDAY	morning afternoon night
FRIDAY	morning afternoon night

Interaction 2 **page 87**

Listening and acting out

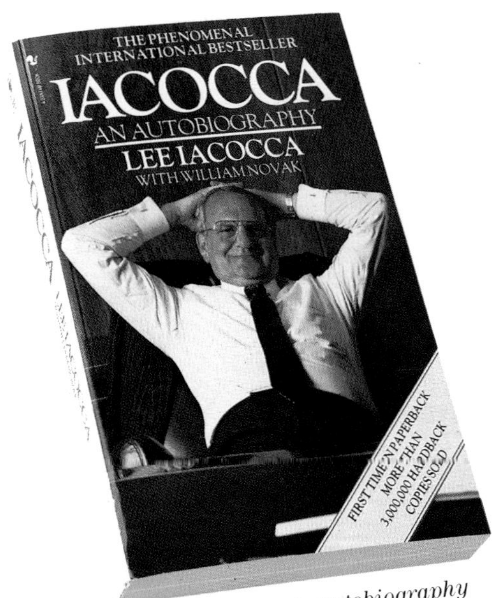

Lee Iacocca's autobiography

Grammar and usage

What's [Carmen] going to do in [September]?
— [She's] going to [visit Italy].

Why is [Antonio] wearing [an apron]?
— Because [he's] going to [cook dinner].

Are you going to take a walk?
Would you [buy me some toothpaste]?

17 Matt's story

POLICEMAN: Now, Mr. Jackson, can you tell me what happened?
MATT: I was on my way to the ball park. Suddenly two men grabbed me and pushed me into a car.
POLICEMAN: What did you do?
MATT: Well . . . they had a gun. They tied my hands. They drove about three hours. Then they stopped and we all got out.
POLICEMAN: I see. Then what did they do?
MATT: They threw me over a cliff. Luckily, Mr. Shubin's dog found me!

1

Look and listen. Answer the questions.

1 Who is telling the story?
2 Put the following actions in the order in which they happen in the story.

tied	grabbed	found	threw
pushed	stopped	drove	got out

Language focus

2

Match the actions below with the pictures of Sofia's activities last week.

listened to music	visited her grandmother
bought a TV	cooked dinner
went shopping	watched TV
read the newspaper	drove to Verona

A.M.	P.M.

Monday

Tuesday

Wednesday

Thursday

3

Ask and answer, like this:

> What did Sofia do on Monday morning?
> — She went shopping.

4

Ask and answer about you, like this:

What did you do last night?
— I watched TV, and then I went to bed.

17

Lisa's day

Language focus

1

Read the text on the right and look at the pictures.

Friday 13th
Tomorrow I'm going to buy some new shoes, read a medical journal, write a report, cook spaghetti, watch TV and take a bath.

Saturday 14th

2

Ask and answer, like this:

> Did Lisa read a medical journal on Saturday?
> — No, she didn't.
> What did she read, then?
> — A magazine.
> Did Lisa watch TV?
> — Yes, she did.

Read and write

3

Read Joan's card to her mother and answer the questions.

1 Where did Bud and Joan drive to on Sunday?

2 What did they do yesterday?

3 Where did they go last night?

4 Where are they going tomorrow?

4

Write your own vacation postcard. Say what you are going to do.

Hi Mom!

Bud and I are having a great time here. On Sunday we drove from Puebla to Veracruz. We spent the day on the beach yesterday. Last night we went to a concert in the open air beside a lake. It was beautiful.

Tomorrow we're on the road again. We're going to drive to Tampico. We'll write again soon.

Love,

Joan and Bud

Mrs. G. Johnson
67 Summerhill Avenue
Toronto
Ontario
Canada M4T 1A9

Veracruz: La Playa, The Beach.

17 After the show

What did you think of the show?

I thought it was awful.

So did I.

Oh, really? I didn't. I thought it was pretty good.

Conversation practice

1

Look and listen.

2

Have similar conversations, like this:

What did you think of ....?	
I thought it was	
So did I.	I didn't. I thought it was ....

Here are some words you can use:

the play

the movie

the book

the dinner

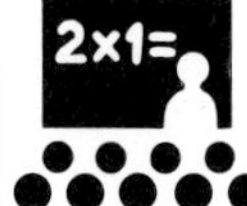

the class

excellent	terrible
fantastic	horrible
great	awful
wonderful	(very) boring
(pretty) good	
(very) interesting	

Review

3

You are talking with Hans.

YOU: ....?
HANS: No, I wasn't at home. I was at the movies.
YOU: ....?
HANS: I saw an old Hitchcock movie — *The Birds*.
YOU: ....?
HANS: Like it? Yes, I thought it was great.
YOU: ....?
HANS: Tonight? I don't know. I'm not going to do anything special.
YOU: ....?
HANS: Near here? No, there isn't a Chinese restaurant, but there's a good pizza parlor.
YOU: ....?
HANS: Yes, I have some money.
YOU: ....?
HANS: Borrow some? All right.
YOU: Now I can take you to the pizza parlor!

Reading

1

Read the following questions. Then answer them by reading the text.

1 Why did Henry Ford hire the expert?
2 Why didn't the expert like one of the employees?
3 Why did Ford like him?

Once Henry Ford hired an efficiency expert to evaluate his car company. After a few weeks, Ford received the report. There was only one problem. The expert mentioned a certain employee and said:

"Every time I go by his office, he's just sitting there, with his feet on his desk, relaxing! He's wasting time and money!"

Ford replied:

"That man once had an idea which saved us several million dollars. His feet were on his desk then, too!"

Interaction 1

Find someone who/whose:

a took a photograph last week ....
b wore a suit two days ago ....
c went skiing last winter ....
d is going to go camping this summer ....
e collects stamps ....
f always reads in bed ....
g is going to watch TV tonight ....
h father can play golf ....
i knows your teacher's favorite food ....

Interaction 2 page 88

Interaction 3

Listening and acting out

Grammar and usage

What did [Sofia] do [on Wednesday afternoon]?
— She [watched TV].
Did [Lisa] [cook spaghetti] [on Saturday]?
Yes, she did./No, she didn't. (= did not)
What did she [cook], then?

What did you think of the [show]?
— I thought it was [awful].
— So did I./I didn't.

18 The big game

MARIA: You made a quick recovery, Matt! Only three days in the hospital!
MATT: I was in good shape.
MARIA: Really! How did you survive?
MATT: I was very, very lucky. I landed on my feet and later untied the ropes. But Yipps is the real hero.
MARIA: How long were you there?
MATT: Two days.
MARIA: Two days! Any idea who did it?
MATT: Two men. But I don't know who they were.
MARIA: But why? Why did they want to get rid of you?
MATT: I don't know. Because of the big game, maybe.
MARIA: Well, we're happy you're safe.
MATT: Thank you.
MARIA: This is Maria Rossi, ABC-TV Sydney, reporting from San Francisco.

1

Look and listen. Answer the questions.

1 How many days was Matt in the hospital?
2 Why did Matt make a quick recovery?
3 How did he survive?

Language focus

2

Study the information on the right.

3

Ask and answer, like this:

> Who wrote *The Grapes of Wrath*?
> — John Steinbeck.

West Side Story
Composer:
Leonard Bernstein

The Grapes of Wrath
Writer:
John Steinbeck

The Mona Lisa
Painter:
Leonardo Da Vinci

4

Ask and answer, like this:

Who acted in *Gone with the Wind*?
— Clark Gable and Vivien Leigh.
— I have no idea! Tell me.

The telephone
Inventor:
Alexander Graham Bell

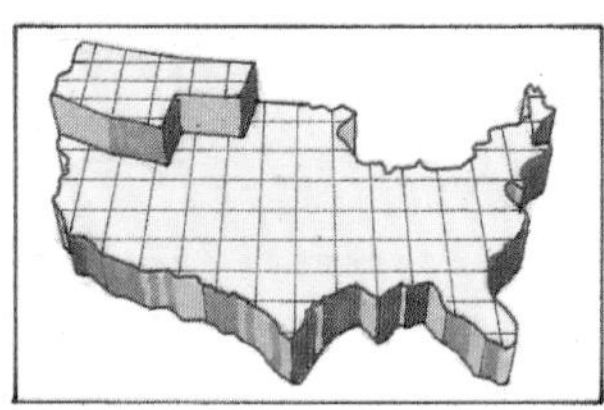

The northwest U.S.A.
Explorers:
Lewis and Clark

Marin County Civic Center
Designer:
Frank Lloyd Wright

Famous people

18

Language focus

1

Look at the pictures and study the information.

Harriet Beecher Stowe
1811–1896
author of *Uncle Tom's Cabin*

Christopher Columbus
1451–1506
discoverer of America

Buster Keaton
1895–1966
actor in silent movies

Louis Armstrong
1900–1971
jazz musician

Walt Disney 1901–1966
creator of Mickey Mouse

2

Ask and answer, like this:

> Why is Christopher Columbus famous?
> — Because he discovered America.
> When was he born?
> — In 1451.
> When did he die?
> — In 1506.

Read and write

3

Read the following text. Copy and complete the empty chart.

Benjamin Franklin was one of America's most famous citizens. He was born in Boston in 1706. He was a writer, inventor and diplomat. He wrote about hard work and honesty in *Poor Richard's Almanack*. He invented the Franklin Stove, bifocal glasses and the lightning rod. In 1776, he went to France as the first diplomat from the United States. He died in 1790 in Philadelphia.

4

Write a similar paragraph about Mark Twain using the information in the completed chart.

Name

Occupation

Date and place

Examples of

Travels

Died

Name
Mark Twain
(real name Samuel Clemens)

Occupation
one of America's most
famous writers

Date and place of birth
1835, Florida, Missouri
(on the Mississippi River)

Examples of work
The Adventures of Huckleberry Finn
The Adventures of Tom Sawyer
(about life on the Mississippi)

Travels
1861 - went west to California,
wrote The Celebrated Jumping Frog
of Calaveras County
1869 - went to Europe,
wrote Innocents Abroad

Died
1910, Redding, Connecticut

18 What happened?

Conversation practice

1

Look and listen.

2

Have similar conversations, like this:

Hi, ...
I'm sorry I ....
What happened?
....
Oh well! ....

Here are some ideas to help you.

Event	Reason	Possible replies
didn't come to your party	a headache	maybe next time
left early	an appointment	it doesn't matter
didn't call you	very busy	don't worry
didn't arrive on time	got lost	that's OK
missed the meeting	train was late	

Review

3

You are talking with Fumiko.

FUMIKO: Did you study English last night?
YOU: ....
FUMIKO: What did you do, then?
YOU: ....
FUMIKO: Oh, really? Do you always do that in the evening?
YOU: ....
FUMIKO: What did you think of today's class?
YOU: ....
FUMIKO: So did I! What are you going to do this weekend?
YOU: ....
FUMIKO: When are you going to be at home?
YOU: ....
FUMIKO: Could you call me then?
YOU: ....
FUMIKO: Great! See you soon!

Reading

1

Read the following questions. Then answer them by reading the text.

1 Why did the motorist stop?
2 What did the first jogger want?
3 Why did the motorist put the note in the window?

A sleepy motorist stopped along a road to take a nap. After a little while, a jogger knocked on the window and asked for the time. The drowsy man said, "It's 8 o'clock." He went back to sleep, and then a while later another jogger knocked on the window. "Do you have the time?" The tired man grumbled, "8:30!" He didn't want it to happen again, so he wrote a note and put it in the window. It read, "I don't have the time." A few minutes later, another jogger came by and knocked on the window. "Hey, mister!" the jogger said. "It's 8:45!"

Interaction 1

This is the story of San Francisco. Put the sentences in the correct order. Use numbers. The first one is done for you.

- [ ] Gold prospectors came from all over the world.
- [ ] The first pioneers came and built the first permanent houses.
- [1] The Spanish explorer sailed up the coast.
- [ ] Some prospectors became rich.
- [ ] Now, there's a modern city on the bay.
- [ ] The new bankers paid for a new railroad.
- [ ] He discovered a beautiful bay.
- [ ] One day, some lumberjacks found gold.
- [ ] The new railroad brought more pioneers.
- [ ] Some of the rich men opened the first banks.

Interaction 2 **page 89**

Listening and acting out

Grammar and usage

Who [invented] the [telephone]?
— [Alexander Graham Bell].

Why is [Mark Twain] famous?
— Because [he] [wrote many novels].
When was [he] born?
— In [1835].
When did [he] die?
— In [1910].
— I have no idea!

I'm sorry I'm late.
— What happened?
— Oh well. Better late than never./It doesn't matter.

19 A phone call

MARC: Hello.
MARIA: Hello, Marc?
MARC: Maria! Where are you?
MARIA: I'm at the hotel. Listen, I have to tell you something.
MARC: Oh? What?
MARIA: I'm flying to L.A. tomorrow, and then next week I have to start a new assignment in Brazil.
MARC: What? Why?
MARIA: Because I have to.
MARC: But Maria . . .
MARIA: Look, Marc, I'm sorry. I don't want to leave San Francisco or say goodbye to you. I'd like to stay.
MARC: Well, then stay!
MARIA: I can't. I have to finish my assignment in California and move on.
MARC: I'd like to see you. Can I come over right now?
MARIA: Oh, Marc. I have to pack. I'll see you before I leave tomorrow.

1 

Look and listen. Answer the questions.

1 Where is Maria flying to?
2 What would she like to do?
3 What does she have to do?

Language focus

2

Match the following descriptions with the pictures.

1 travel around the world
2 wash the dishes
3 meet interesting people
4 translate business letters
5 make the beds
6 talk with clients
7 study philosophy

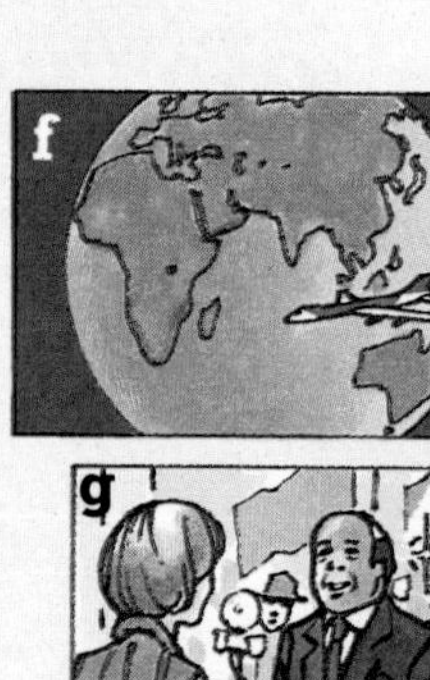

3

Ask and answer, like this:

> What does Diane have to do at work?
> — She has to type letters.
> What would she like to do?
> — She'd like to travel around the world.

4

Ask and answer about you, like this:

What do you have to do at work?
— I have to write reports and talk with clients.
What would you like to do?
— I'd like to visit China.

19

What's the matter?

Language focus

1

Look at the pictures and study the information.

2

Ask and answer, like this:

> What's the matter with the man with the beard?
> — He has to go out, but he doesn't want to get wet.

Read and write

3

Read this text and answer the questions.

1 What does Jerry Jenson do?
2 What does Jerry like about his job?
3 Where does he have to spend three weeks every month?
4 Where does he have to eat?
5 What would Jerry like to do?
6 Does Jerry's wife like his plans?

Jerry Jenson is a petroleum engineer from Long Beach, California. He works on a platform near Jakarta, Indonesia. His family lives in Jakarta. He likes his salary and his work, but there are some things about his job that he doesn't like. He has to spend three weeks every month on the platform, and he always has to eat in the company cafeteria.

He would like to go back to California to live a regular life with his family. He wants to go windsurfing with his son and have weekend barbecues with his friends. Jerry's wife also wants to live in the States again.

4

Write a paragraph about what you do, like this:

I am a(n) . . . . but there are a couple of things about my job that I don't like.
I have to . . . . and I always have to . . . .
I would like to . . . . I want to . . . .

Conversation practice

1

Look and listen.

2

Have similar conversations, like this:

Would you like to ....?	
Oh, I can't . . . I have to	Yes, that would be great!
How about ...., then?	
Yes, that would be great!	Actually, I'm busy then, too. Maybe some other time.

Here are some ideas:

Would you like to . . . ?	*I have to . . .*
go out to dinner take a walk in the park go to the theater go out for a drink go out for coffee	get home wash my hair call my brother do some work get up early tomorrow

Review

3

You are talking with Felipe.

YOU: ....?
FELIPE: I feel awful!
YOU: ....?
FELIPE: I went jogging this morning in the rain.
YOU: ....?
FELIPE: Yes, I got very wet.
YOU: ....?
FELIPE: Tomorrow? No, I'm not going to get wet again.
YOU: ....?
FELIPE: No, I don't have any aspirin. That's why I feel awful.
YOU: ....?
FELIPE: Coffee? Yes, I'd love some.
YOU: ....?
FELIPE: With cream and sugar, please. Thank you.
YOU: ....

Reading

1

Read the following questions. Then answer them by reading the text.

1 What happened to Buzz Brooks last night?
2 What did his customers bet on?
3 What did the police find?

BOOKIE ARRESTED

The Press Syndicate

San Francisco, CA — The police arrested Buzz Brooks last night at his Nob Hill home. They charged him with operating an illegal gambling organization. His "customers" bet on everything from horses to golf. But the bets were always high — $2,000 or more. Police found $2,000,000 in cash and records of all the bets in the office vault.

Police Chief Martin O'Brien said, "It's only the beginning. A lot of important people aren't going to sleep very well tonight."

Interaction 1

Make a chart like the one below. Ask other students what they have to do at home and at work/school. Ask what they would like to do in the future, too.

Name	
have to do	*work*
	home
would like to do	*work*
	personal

Interaction 2 **page 90**

Interaction 3

Listening and acting out

Grammar and usage

What does [Diane] have to do [at home]?
— She has to [wash the dishes].
What would [Diane] like to do?
— She'd like to [study philosophy]. (= She would)
What's the matter with [the man]?
— He has to [go out], but he doesn't want to [get wet].

Would you like to [go out for dinner]?
— Oh, I can't . . . /That would be great.
How about tomorrow?

20 The winners

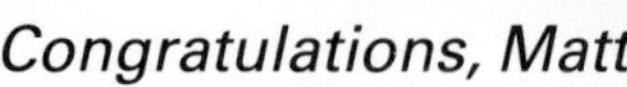

RON: Congratulations, Matt! That was a fantastic game.
MATT: Fantastic for us. But not for you, huh, Ron?
RON: What? What do you mean? I . . .
MATT: You bet on the Green Sox, didn't you? Forty thousand dollars.
RON: I . . . I . . .
MATT: And you told those gangsters all about me, didn't you?
RON: I . . . I . . . thought . . . it was just for a few days . . .
MATT: So I was right.
RON: But you're safe now. You're not going to turn me in, are you?
POLICEMAN: He doesn't have to. We already know your story. In fact, *we* told Matt. Let's go.

1

Look and listen. Answer the questions.

1 Did the Seals win the game?
2 Who did Ron Bellugi bet on?
3 Who told Matt about Bellugi?

Language focus

2

Who are these people?

a

b

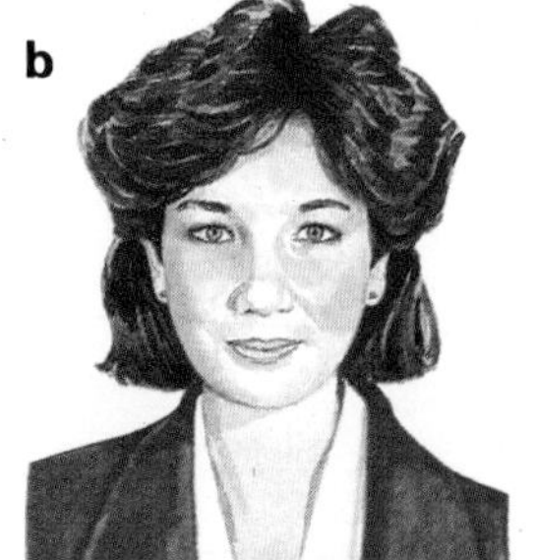

c

d

e

f

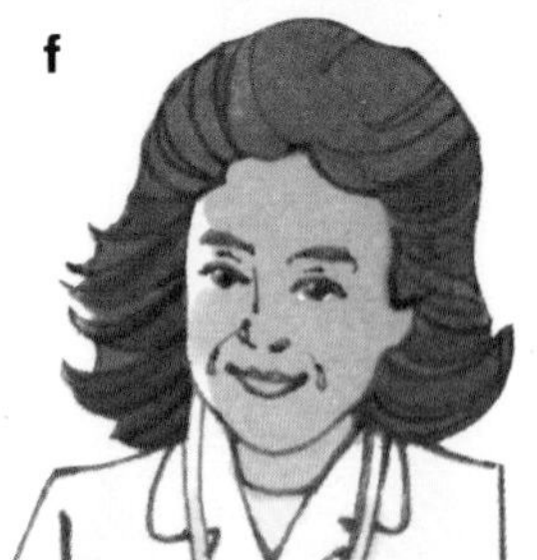

3

Try to remember the characters. Then ask and answer questions, like this:

Lisa's American, isn't she?
— Yes, she is.
Carol lost her dog, didn't she?
— Yes, she did.

4

Ask and answer about you, like this:

You're Mexican, aren't you?
— Yes, I am.
You can speak Spanish, can't you?
— Yes, of course!

Sylvie's vacation

Language focus

1

Read this about Sylvie and look at the pictures.

Sylvie is on vacation. Yesterday she said, "Tomorrow I'm going to get up early and go swimming. Before lunch I'm going to take some pictures. In the afternoon, I'm going to lie in the sun and write postcards. In the evening, I'm going to watch TV."

Now it's the afternoon. Sylvie isn't writing postcards, and she can't lie in the sun. She isn't going to watch TV tonight. In the morning she didn't get up early, she didn't go swimming and she didn't take any pictures.

reading a book

overslept

TV

2

Ask and answer, like this:

> Why didn't Sylvie take any pictures this morning?
> — Because she dropped her camera.
> Why can't Sylvie lie in the sun?
> — Because she's sunburned.

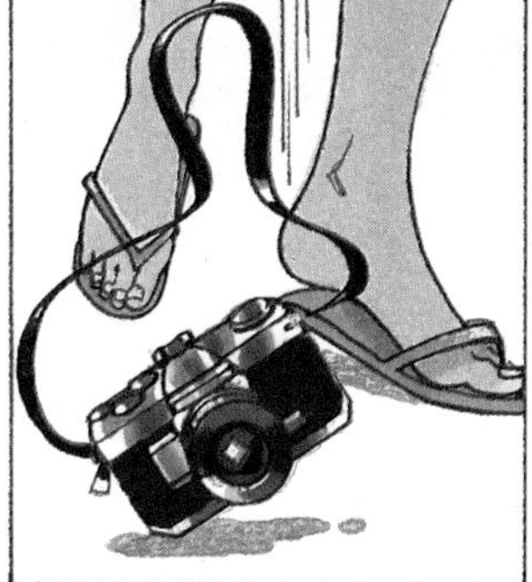
dropped her camera

sunburned

cold water

Read and write

3

Study the chart on the right. Then write two paragraphs about "X."

Name:	"X"
Age:	33
Nationality:	American
Permanent address:	unknown
Temporary address:	Cell 23, San Quentin Prison, California
Duties:	peeling potatoes, making license plates
Description:	tall, thin, moustache, scar on left cheek
Likes:	motor boats, tropical climates
Dislikes:	potatoes, license plates
Weekend activities:	peeling potatoes, watching baseball games on TV

20 Take care!

Conversation practice

1

Look and listen.

2

Have similar conversations, like this:

Thank you for ....
Our pleasure. We enjoyed ....
Well, goodbye. I'll ....
We'll .... Goodbye.

Here are some ideas to help you:

Thanks for		Possible replies
a wonderful	party	seeing you
	dinner	talking to you
	evening	having you
inviting me		

Promises	Possible replies
give you a call be in touch/keep in touch	wait to hear from you, then
see you soon	look forward to that

Review

3

You are talking with Fumiko.

FUMIKO: Well, that's the end of our English course! Did you like your English classes?
YOU: ....
FUMIKO: What are you going to do now that the course is over?
YOU: ....
FUMIKO: Would you like to come to a farewell party at school tonight?
YOU: ....
FUMIKO: That's too bad. What do you have to do?
YOU: ....
FUMIKO: How about tomorrow for coffee?
YOU: ....
FUMIKO: OK. See you then!
YOU: ....

Reading

1

Read the following questions. Then answer them by reading the text.

1 Why do more people speak English today?

2 How do American English and British English differ?

3 Are there any other reasons why English is growing as an international language? Discuss.

English — an international language

Most languages borrow words from others. The French talk about *le weekend*, and the Italians use the word *paprika* (from Hungarian). The Japanese talk about *arbeito* (from German), meaning a part-time job. But today most of the borrowed words are from English. And today more people speak English than before. Why is this?

There are several reasons. One is the increase in scientific information printed in English. Eighty per cent of scientific discoveries are reported in English. Also, most international news agencies send reports in English all over the world.

A lot of international businesspeople use English daily. When a Mexican businessman buys from a Thai manufacturer, or a Brazilian exporter sells to a German importer, English is probably used.

There are many dialects of English, but the two major groups are American English and British English. Although they sometimes differ in pronunciation and usage (for example, Americans say *apartments, cookies* and *you're welcome*, while Britons say *flats, biscuits* and *not at all*), they are the same language. So, for whatever reason you're learning English, you can be sure that it's going to be useful all over the world.

Japanese soda cans, showing a mixture of Japanese and English

An air traffic controller at work: English is the international language of the air

Interaction 1 page 91
Interaction 2
Listening and acting out

Grammar and usage

He's [American], isn't he?
She [lost her dog], didn't she?
Why didn't [Sylvie] [take any pictures] [this morning]?
— Because she [dropped her camera].

We enjoyed seeing you.	Our pleasure.
I'll give you a call.	
We'll look forward to that.	Take care.

1

Interaction 1

Look at the pictures. Put the words below in the right balloons.

(In Los Angeles.) (Hello.) (Where do you live?)

(What's your name?) (What do you do?)

Interaction 2

1 Student **A** says his/her work phone number, home phone number, etc. Student **B** writes them down.

2 Now change. Student **B** says the numbers, and student **A** writes them down.

Listening and acting out

1

Who is the patient — **a**, **b** or **c**?

a Anne:	teacher	Paris, Texas
b James:	businessman	London, Kentucky
c Laura:	student	Moscow, California

2

Have conversations like the one on the cassette. Student **A** is a doctor, student **B** a patient. Student **A** asks **B** about his/her occupation. Student **A** fills in the form below about **B**.

NAME: __________

HOME: __________

OCCUPATION: __________

Interaction 1

Read the text and fill in Jerry's family tree.

Hi! My name is Jerry. My wife's name is Brenda. We have two sons (Bob and David) and a daughter, Laurie. My father, Frank, is retired and my mother, Martha, is a dentist. My sister, Nancy, is in Mexico now and my brother, Sam, is at my parents' home. He isn't married.

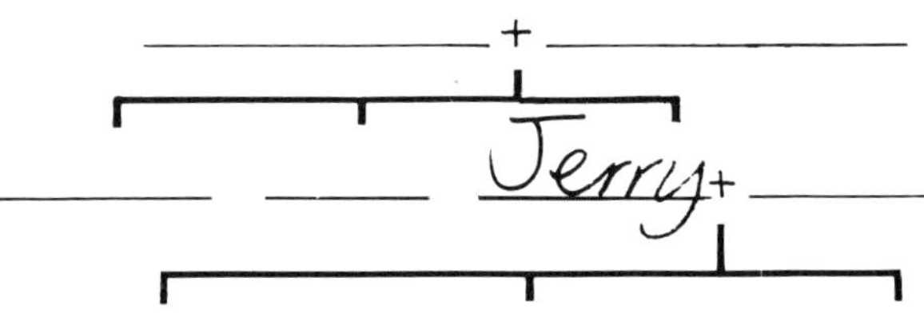

Interaction 2

Name	*John*	*Ann*	*Tim*	*Sue*
Home		*Honolulu*		*Montreal*
Occupation	*accountant*			*nurse*
Now		*at home*	*at work*	

▲ STUDENT A

Ask and answer questions to complete the charts. Do not look at your partner's chart! *For example:*

A: Where does John live?
B: In Sydney.

▼ STUDENT B

Name	*John*	*Ann*	*Tim*	*Sue*
Home	*Sydney*		*Washing-ton, D.C.*	
Occupation		*teacher*	*librarian*	
Now	*at work*			*at work*

Listening and acting out

1

Who is the girl in the picture? (Kim or Jane?)

2

Write *Jane*, *her mother* and *her father* under the correct pictures.

3

Have conversations like the one on the cassette.

Ask if someone is there.
Ask where they are.

Interaction 1

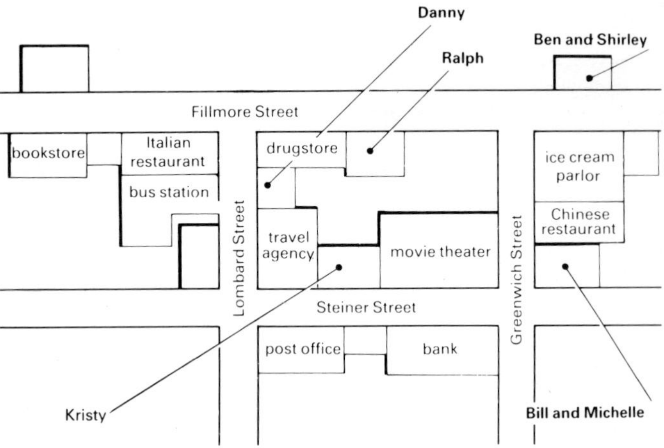

Ask about: Jim, Kathleen, Carl and Amy, Tracy, Scott and Joanne.
Write their names on the map.

▲ STUDENT A

Ask and answer questions to find where the people live. Do not look at your partner's map!
For example:

A: Where does Jim live?
B: Across the street from the bookstore.

▼ STUDENT B

Ask about: Kristy, Ben and Shirley, Danny, Ralph, Bill and Michelle.
Write their names on the map.

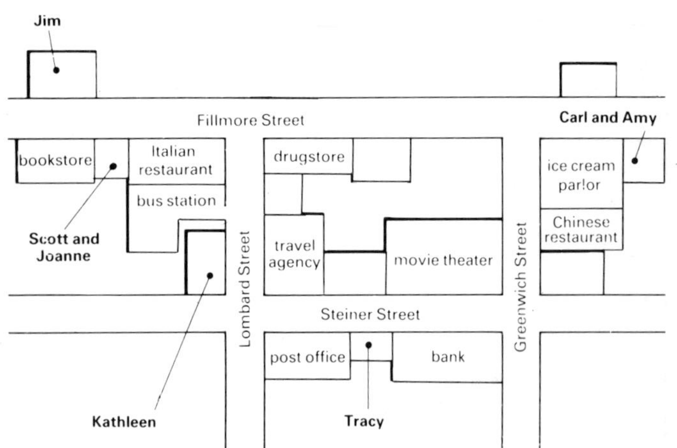

Listening and acting out

1

Say whether the statements are true or false.

1 Her father is a doctor.
2 Her mother is a doctor.
3 The man is a policeman.

2

Look at the map. Put an **X** for the hospital.

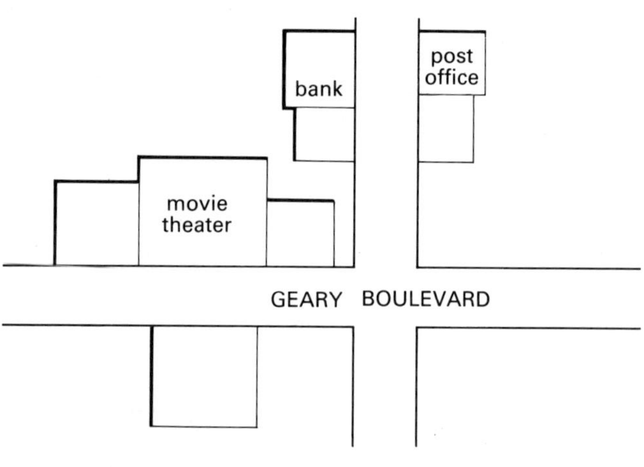

3

Student **A** is a child. He/she is at home, but his/her father/mother/sister etc. are not at home. Student **B** is doing a survey and arrives at **A**'s home. Student **B** asks about **A**'s father/mother etc., and their jobs. Where are they now?

Interaction 1

1 Your teacher will say a number.
2 Put an **X** on that number
3 When you have 3 **X**s in a line, call "Bingo!"

				A						C	
Example:			16	70	15		B		19	30	40
~~16~~	12	15	17	13	30	18	12	80	13	15	90
13	~~50~~	~~20~~	60	50	12	13	15	50	14	50	11
14	60	~~40~~				30	40	14			

4 Now do the same in groups. Use a new piece of paper and make new boxes. Choose one person to say the numbers.

Interaction 2

NAME	James O'Reilly	Mr. Shubin	Barbara Steiger	Jin Wong	Student B's brother/sister
NATION-ALITY	Irish		German		
AGE		68		35	
OCCUPA-TION	musician		dancer		
HOME	Dublin		Munich		

▲ STUDENT A

Ask and answer questions to complete the charts. Do not look at your partner's chart!
For example:

A: How old is James O'Reilly?
B: He's twenty.
B: Where's he from?
A: He's from Dublin.
B: Is he Irish?
A: Yes, he is.

▼ STUDENT B

NAME	James O'Reilly	Mr. Shubin	Barbara Steiger	Jin Wong	Student A's brother/sister
NATION-ALITY		American		Chinese	
AGE	20		31		
OCCUPA-TION		lawyer		engineer	
HOME		Arizona		Beijing	

Listening and acting out

Ray, Patty, Mike and Sam are at a party.

1

Listen to the cassette and put the sentences in the correct order. (Put the numbers 1, 2 or 3 in the boxes.)

RAY: Mike, this is Patty. ☐
RAY: Hi. I'm Ray. ☐
PATTY: Sam, let me introduce Ray and Mike. ☐

2

Listen to the cassette again. Say whether the statements are true or false.

1 Ray is American. T F
2 Patty is Australian. T F
3 Patty lives in San Francisco. T F
4 Patty is a designer. T F
5 Patty is twenty-five years old. T F

3

You are at a party, and you do not know anybody.
You can talk about: name
home
occupation
nationality

Interaction 1

Look at the pictures. Put the words below in the right balloons.

Sergio. | Where's he from? | He's a pilot. | Where were you last night? | Italy.

Interaction 2

Choose someone in the class and complete this chart about him/her.

NAME: .... AGE: ....

HOME: ....

OCCUPATION: ....

NATIONALITY: ....

WHERE?

1 ten o'clock yesterday morning

....

2 three o'clock yesterday afternoon

....

3 five o'clock yesterday afternoon

....

4 nine o'clock last night

....

Listening and acting out

1

Listen to the cassette and answer the questions.

1 Where was Charlie:
 - **a** at nine o'clock?
 - **b** at ten o'clock?

2 Who was Charlie with:
 - **a** at nine o'clock?
 - **b** at ten o'clock?

2

Look. This was the bank at 10 o'clock last night.

Student **A** is a policeman. Ask the others about last night. Were they the thieves?

6

Interaction 1

1 Everyone puts 1, 2 or 3 things on a desk at the front of the room.
2 One student stands at the desk.
3 Ask and answer, like this:

Interaction 2

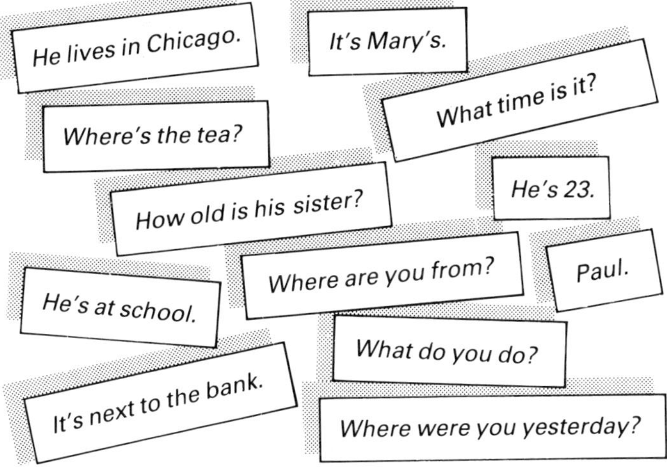

▲ STUDENT A

Work in pairs to match the questions and answers. Don't look at your partner's questions or answers.*

▼ STUDENT B

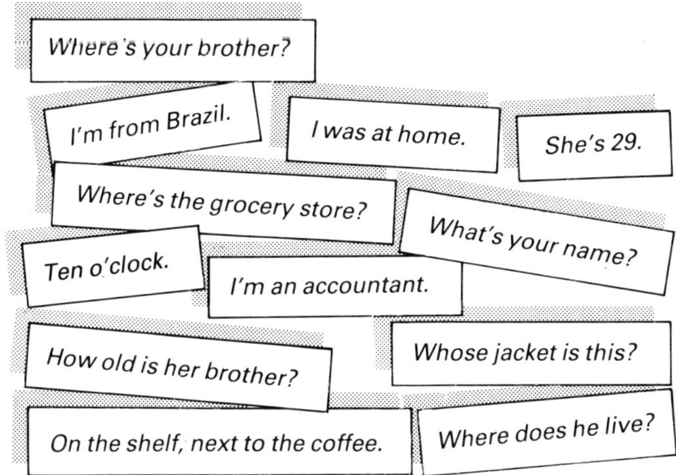

*See Teacher's Manual for alternative presentation.

Listening and acting out

1

Listen to the cassette and answer the questions.

1 Where are Lester and Joyce?
2 Whose hat is it?
3 Whose coat is it?
4 Whose party is it?

2

Choose the correct answers.

1 What time is it?
   a ten o'clock
   b eleven o'clock
   c twelve o'clock

2 Where were Joyce's gloves?

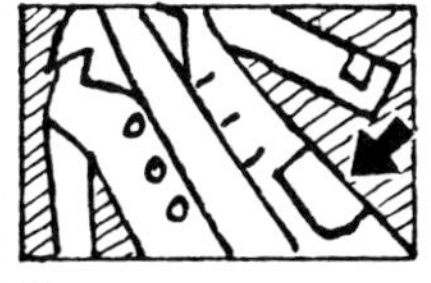
a

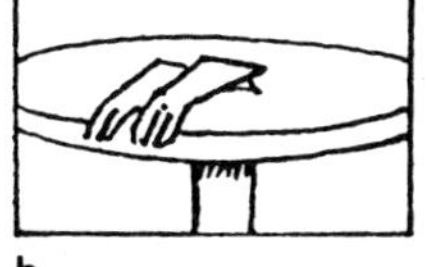
b

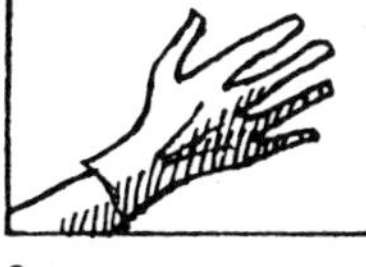
c

3

At the end of a party, you go home.
Talk about the time.
Get your hats, coats and gloves.
Say goodbye and thank you.

Interaction 1

You own a large department store. You have only one kind of item in each department. Check (√) the item you have in each department. Now ask your partner about the items they have in their store.

Department	Items	You	Your partner
TVs	color		
	black and white		
Calculators	pocket		
	desk top		
Software	computer games		
	business software		
Typewriters	electronic		
	manual		
Freezers	refrigerator		
	freezer		
Music	record player		
	cassette recorder		

Interaction 2

Find someone who/whose:

a has a French dictionary ....
b was at the movies last night ....
c birthday was last month ....
d has some car keys in his/her pocket ....
e has a chess game ....
f mother is a nurse ....
g has some nephews ....
h father has a Japanese car ....
i wasn't at home last night ....

Listening and acting out

1

Listen to the cassette. Check (√) the correct answer or answers.

1 Bev and Rich are in
______ Mexico City
______ Portland
______ Acapulco

2 Rich would like
______ a steak
______ a hamburger
______ a fishburger
______ a Mexican omelette

3 They don't have any
______ steaks
______ hamburgers
______ fishburgers
______ Mexican omelettes

4 They have
______ steaks
______ hamburgers
______ omelettes
______ salads

2

Listen again and answer the questions.

1 Where were Rich and Bev yesterday?
2 What would Rich like for dinner?

3

Now you're out to dinner. Use the dishes above as a menu. Student **A** is a waiter/waitress. Students **B** and **C** are customers. Have a nice dinner!

Interaction 2

8.30

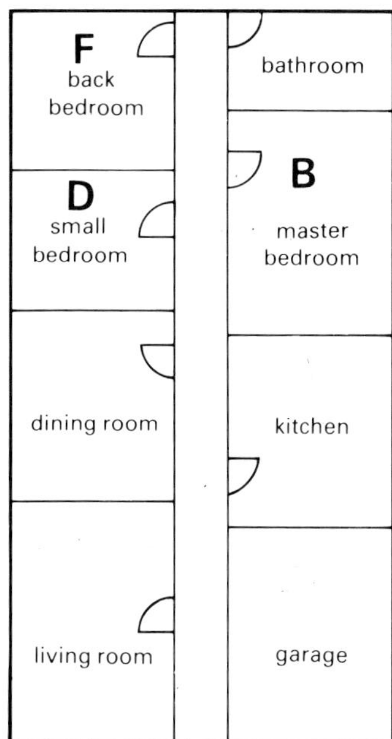

10.45

▲ STUDENT A

This is the Johnsons' house at 8:30 and 10:45 in the evening. Find out where A) Alan, B) Barbara, C) Claire, D) Doris, E) Edward and F) Frank were at 8:30 or 10:45. Do not look at your partner's chart. *For example:*

A: Where was Alan at 8:30?
B: He was in the kitchen.

▼ STUDENT B

8.30

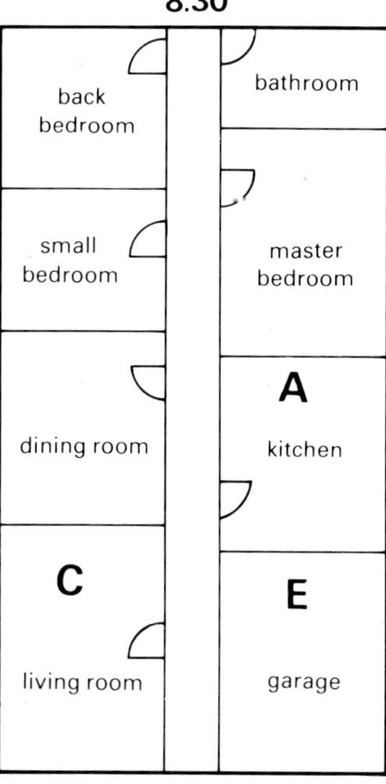

10.45

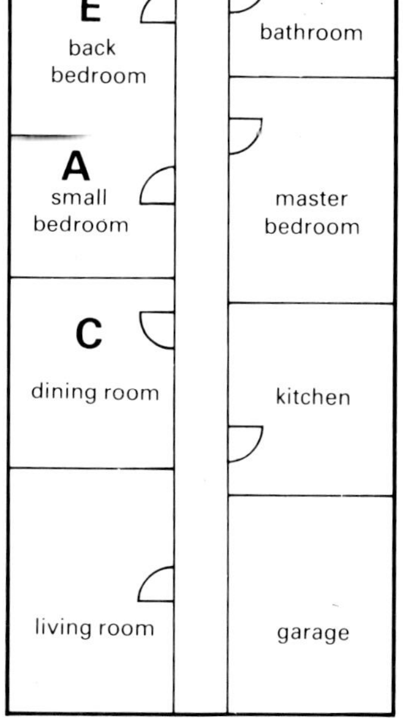

Listening and acting out

1

Listen to the cassette and answer the questions.

1 Where does Mr. Simpson want to go?
2 Which of the following tours/excursions are mentioned?

__ **a** Yosemite ski tour
__ **b** Disneyland weekend
__ **c** Redwoods tour
__ **d** California coast tour
__ **e** special wine tour
__ **f** wine country tour
__ **g** Silicon Valley tour
__ **h** Lake Tahoe ski trip

2

Listen again and indicate tour/excursion dates. For example:

The wine country tour (f) is on the 7th, 14th, 21st and 28th February.

FEBRUARY						
SUN	MON	TUES	WED	THURS	FRI	SAT
	1	2	3	4	5	6
f 7	8	9	10	11	12	13
f 14	15	16	17	18	19	20
f 21	22	23	24	25	26	27
f 28	1	2	3	4	5	6

3

Student **A** is a travel agent. Student **B** calls to book an excursion. Talk about dates and destinations, and choose your excursion.

Interaction 1

NAME	Bill Brockus	Kurt Pitt	Ernie West
JOB	pilot	coach	doctor
HOBBY	collecting antiques	dancing	traveling
SPORT	tennis	baseball	sailing
MUSIC	jazz	classical	country and western
FOOD	hamburgers	Japanese	spaghetti

▲ STUDENT A

You and your partner have an important dinner party. Student **A** has 3 guests, **Bill**, **Kurt**, and **Ernie**, and student **B** had 3 guests, **Angela**, **Nancy**, and **Jill**.

The guests don't know each other. Copy the grid on the right. Ask your partner about his/her guests and put the information in the grid. Then arrange the seats. Don't forget your seat!

NAME	JOB	HOBBY	SPORT	MUSIC	FOOD

▼ STUDENT B

NAME	Angela Witt	Nancy Wells	Jill Newt
JOB	accountant	nurse	lawyer
HOBBY	dancing	photography	collecting coins
SPORT	softball	water skiing	tennis
MUSIC	opera	folk	blues
FOOD	rice and vegetables	pizza	hot dogs

Listening and acting out

1

Listen to the cassette and answer the questions.

1 What does Steve Berstein do?
2 Where is he from originally?
3 Where does he live now?

2

Listen to the cassette again and say whether the statements are true or false.

1 Steve does not like India. T F
2 Steve likes curry. T F
3 Steve likes San Francisco. T F
4 Steve likes his own music. T F

3

Student **A** is a famous person, student **B** is an interviewer on a TV program. **B** asks **A** about his/her home, nationality, likes and dislikes, etc.

10

Interaction 2

FLIGHT NUMBER	DESTINATION	DEPARTURE	ARRIVAL (LT*)
389		6:15	10:15
560			12:00
027	Las Vegas	9:00	
951	Los Angeles		11:15
006		7:00	
323			10:30
*LT = local time			

▲ **STUDENT A**

Ask your partner for the missing flight information and complete the charts. Do not look at your partner's chart!

▼ **STUDENT B**

FLIGHT NUMBER	DESTINATION	DEPARTURE	ARRIVAL (LT*)
389	Denver		
560	Honolulu	8:45	
027			10:30
951		10:00	
006	Portland		8:30
323	San Diego	9:00	
*LT = local time			

Listening and acting out

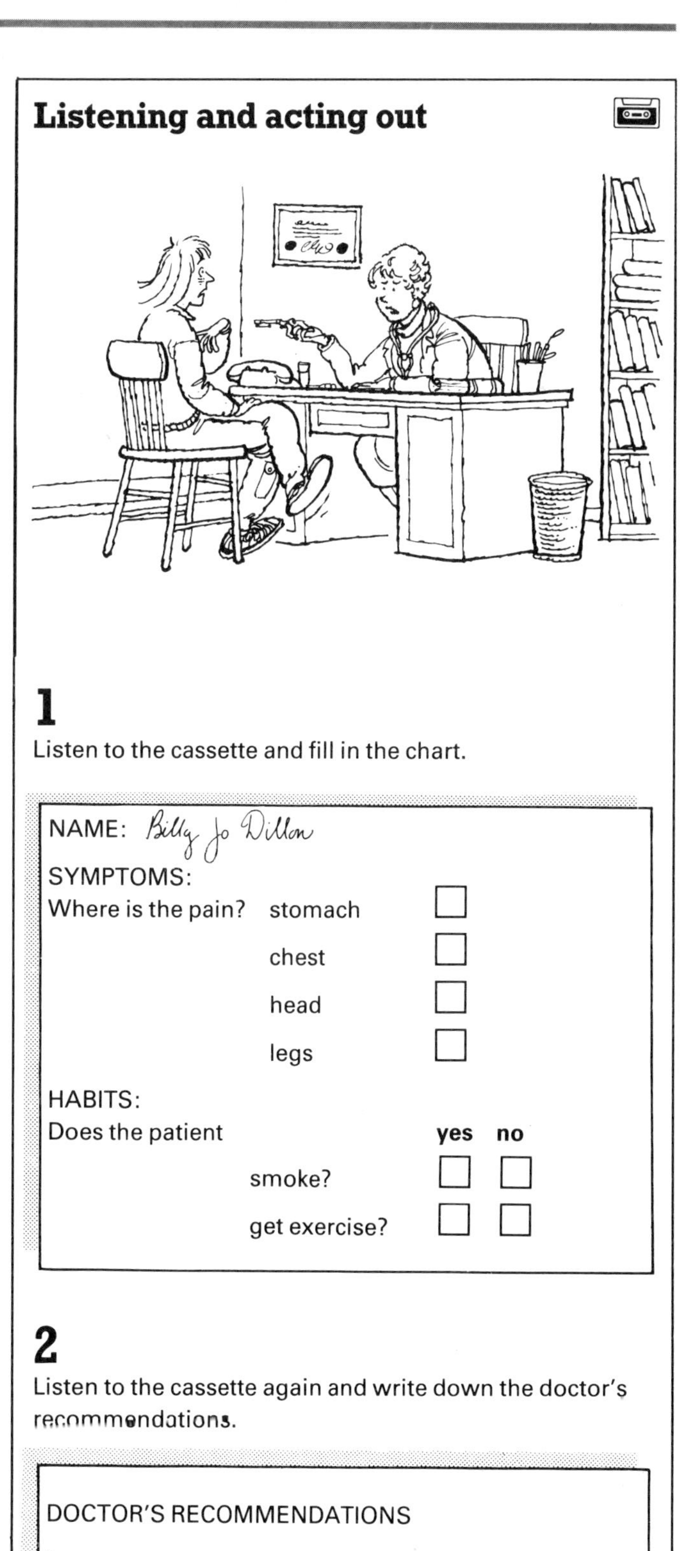

1

Listen to the cassette and fill in the chart.

NAME: Billy Jo Dillon

SYMPTOMS:

Where is the pain? stomach ☐ chest ☐ head ☐ legs ☐

HABITS:

Does the patient

	yes	no
smoke?	☐	☐
get exercise?	☐	☐

2

Listen to the cassette again and write down the doctor's recommendations.

DOCTOR'S RECOMMENDATIONS

1 __________

2 __________

3 __________

3

Have similar conversations. Student **A** is the doctor, student **B** is the patient. The doctor asks the patient about his/her habits. The doctor makes recommendations.

Interaction 1

▲ **STUDENT A** Look at the picture. Color the shoes, pants, sweater, eyes and hair (or write the colors). Ask and answer questions to find similarities between your pictures. Don't
▼ **STUDENT B** look at your partner's picture.

Listening and acting out

1

Match Bruce Stern, Lisa Muller, Candy Richards and Calvin Christoff with their ideal husband or wife.

a a short man with a beard and glasses	**b** a tall thin woman with blue eyes and blond hair
c a tall thin man with gray hair and blue eyes	**d** a short woman with brown eyes and a pleasant face

2

Have similar conversations. Student **A** works at *Find Your Partner*, and student **B** wants a husband/wife. Student **A** asks **B** about the "ideal" husband/wife.

— short/tall?
— how old?
— color of eyes?

12

Interaction 2

No, I don't. I don't smoke.

Can you cook?

Yes, I can. But I don't like cold water.

He's tall and thin with brown hair and glasses.

Where were they yesterday afternoon?

What do you have for breakfast?

Do you like the movies?

Where do you work?

I read or watch TV.

What does his mother look like?

I walk.

Yes, I can. I sing in the shower.

No, they aren't. They're Karl's.

What time is it?

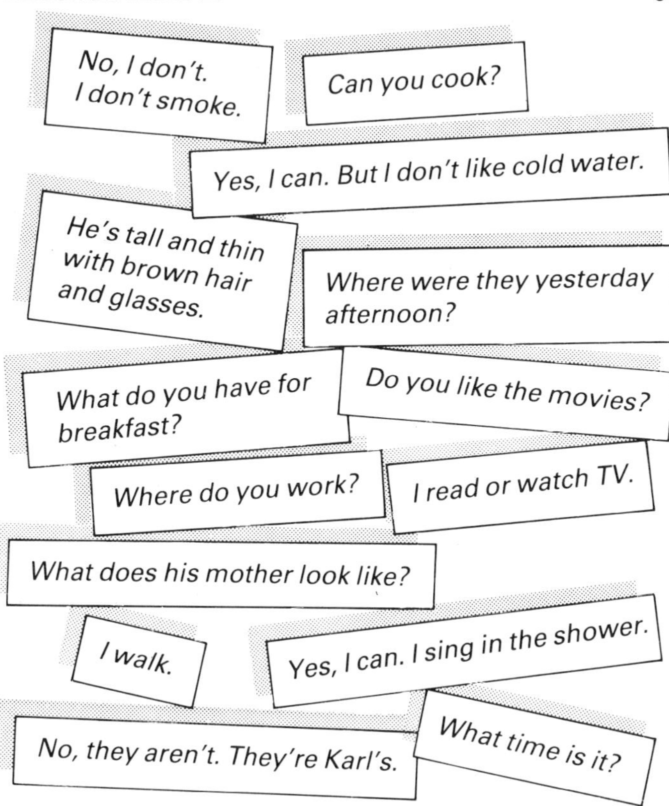

▲ STUDENT A
▼ STUDENT B

Work in pairs to match the questions and answers. Don't look at your partner's questions or answers.*

At a bank.

Do you have a cigarette?

She's average height and weight, with gray hair and blue eyes.

How do you get to work?

Yes, I can. Hamburgers and eggs.

What does he look like?

Can you swim?

I guess they were at work.

Are these your sunglasses?

It's a quarter after 12.

What do you usually do in the evening?

Yes, I go at least once a week.

Can you sing?

An egg, toast and a cup of coffee.

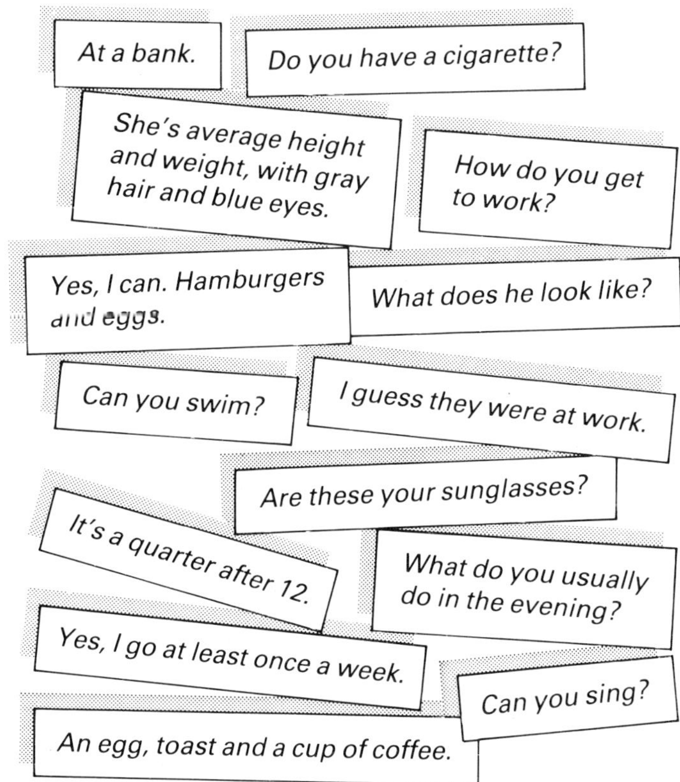

*See Teacher's Manual for alternative presentation.

Listening and acting out

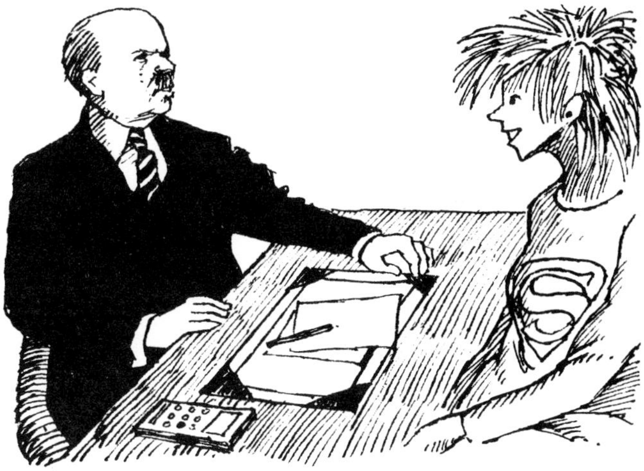

1

Listen to the cassette and say whether the statements are true or false.

1 The man works in a theater.
2 Ms. Novak is a secretary.
3 The man wants a secretary.

2

Listen to the cassette again. Complete this form.

NAME:

ABILITIES:	yes	no
Can type?	☐	☐
Can take shorthand?	☐	☐

OTHER ABILITIES

1 __________
2 __________
3 __________
4 __________

3

Have job interviews. Student **A** wants a job as a secretary. Student **B** interviews student **A** and fills in the form below.

NAME

	yes	no
ABILITIES: Can type?	☐	☐
Can take shorthand?	☐	☐

What languages can he/she speak? . . . .

13

Interaction 1

1 Make two teams, A and B.
2 A member of team A chooses a word and makes a sentence. If it's correct, write A on the word.
3 Then a member of team B chooses a word and makes a sentence. If it's correct, write B on the word.
4 The first team with a straight line wins!

Example:

what (B)	when	where
can	can't (B)	why
often	onions	any (B)

Team B is the winner!

never	often	once
tennis	always	twice
usually	could	how often

hobby	night	weekend
music	TV	exercise
well	badly	concert

Interaction 2

Ask another student about his/her spare time, and fill in the chart below.

Example:
How often do you watch TV?
— About once a week.

Name ______________________

ACTIVITY   HOW OFTEN?

* watch TV ______________________
* listen to music ______________________
* read magazines ______________________
* exercise ______________________
* play cards ______________________
* go to restaurants ______________________
* go to the movies/theater ______________________
* go to concerts ______________________
* (other) ______________________

Listening and acting out

1

Listen to the cassette and answer the questions.

1 Who is Bud Samson?
2 Where are Terry and Bud?
3 What is Bud's hobby?
4 What is Bud's favorite food?

2

Listen to the cassette again. Put Bud's activities with the correct adverb.

always ....
often ....
usually ....

3

In groups of three, have interviews like the one on the cassette. Student **A** is a famous personality. Students **B** and **C** are reporters. They ask **A** about his/her activities, hobbies, likes and dislikes, etc.

Interaction 2

NAME	JOB	NOW / HOW OFTEN
Mandy		
Pauline	actress	eating brunch/ twice a week
Tony and Pat		
Joan and Kate		
Mark and John	teachers	playing softball/ once a week

▲ STUDENT A

Ask and answer questions to complete the charts. Do not look at your partner's chart.

▼ STUDENT B

NAME	JOB	NOW / HOW OFTEN
Mandy	painter	jogging/every morning
Pauline		
Tony and Pat	singers	swimming/once a week
Joan and Kate	dancers	working out / every morning
Mark and John		

Listening and acting out

1

Listen to the cassette and answer the questions.

1 Where is Judy?
2 Who is paying for the call?
3 How does George feel?
4 What is George doing?

2

Put the correct names, Tony, Jane, Marty and George under the pictures.

3

Student **A** calls home. Student **A** asks student **B**:

how he/she is feeling.
how the other people in the house are.
what they are doing.

Interaction 1

BANANA CAKE	RICE PUDDING	APPLE PIE
☐ 2 cups flour	☐ 2 eggs	☐ ½ cup butter
☐ ½ cup sugar	☐ 2 cups milk	☐ 6 apples
☐ 3 eggs	☐ ½ cup yogurt	☐ 2 cups flour
☐ ½ cup butter	☐ ½ teaspoon salt	☐ ½ tea-spoon salt
☐ 2 bananas	☐ 2 cups rice	☐ 1 cup sugar
☐ ½ cup nuts	☐ ½ cup sugar	

▲ STUDENT A

Student **A**: Imagine student **B** is your roommate. You are at work. Friends are coming to dinner. The stores are closed. Which dessert can you make? Call home. Find out what ingredients you have and then decide.
Student **B**: Imagine student **A** is your roommate. You are at home. He/she calls you.

For example:

A: Do we have any eggs?
B: Sure.
A: How many?
B: Two.

Note:
1 cup = ½ pound = 200 grams (solid)
1 cup = ¼ quart = 0.25 liters (liquid)

▼ STUDENT B

CUPBOARD ***REFRIGERATOR***

Listening and acting out

1

Listen to the cassette and answer the questions.

1 Who is selling the house, the man or the woman?
2 How much is the house, according to the newspaper?
3 How much is the house, according to the woman?

2

Listen to the cassette again and write the correct numbers.

Bedrooms ....

Bathrooms ....

Acres (of land) ....

Swimming pools ....

3

Student **B** is selling his/her house.
Student **A** wants information about the house.
Student **A** calls student **B**. Student **A** should ask about the numbers of bedrooms/bathrooms, etc.

Interaction 2

Look at the pictures. Say who you think the people are, what they have, what they *are doing* and what they are *going to do*. Use your dictionary.

Listening and acting out

1

Listen to the cassette and answer the questions.

1 Who is Ernest B. Gold?
2 When is the shuttle going to lift off?
3 What is the main objective of the mission?
4 What is Steve Terelli good at?

2

Complete the mission details.

MISSION DETAILS
Number of crew members: Men: ______________
Women: ______________

Main objective: to ______________ supplies.

Other tasks:

1 ______________ radiation levels.

2 ______________ the moon.

3

Student **A** is going on an expedition to either **a)** the North Pole, or **b)** the sea bed or **c)** a desert island.
Student **A** plans who is going to go on the expedition and what they are going to do.
Student **B** interviews student **A** about the expedition.

17

Interaction 2

Put the sentences in the correct order to make a dialog. The first one is done for you.*

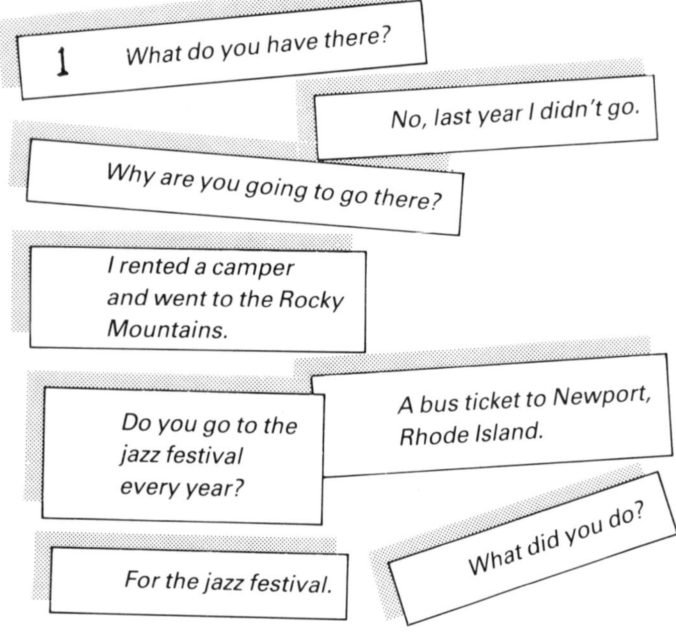

1 What do you have there?

No, last year I didn't go.

Why are you going to go there?

I rented a camper and went to the Rocky Mountains.

Do you go to the jazz festival every year?

A bus ticket to Newport, Rhode Island.

For the jazz festival.

What did you do?

Interaction 3

Work in pairs. Ask each other about past and future trips.

NAME ____________________

LAST TRIP	(destination) ____________________
	(reason for the trip) ____________________
	(activities during the trip) ____________________
NEXT TRIP	(destination) ____________________
	(reason for the trip) ____________________
	(activities during the trip) ____________________

Report back to the class.

*See Teacher's Manual for alternative presentation.

Listening and acting out

1

Listen to the cassette and put these pictures (**a–f**) in the correct order in the box below.

1	2	3	4	5	6

2

Answer the questions.

1 What did Mrs. Jones buy at the drugstore?
2 What was the car like?
3 How many men were there in the car
a when it arrived? **b** when it drove away?
4 What did Mrs. Jones do?

3

Student **A** saw the robbery. Student **B** is the police officer. Student **A** tells the police officer about the robbery.

18

Interaction 2

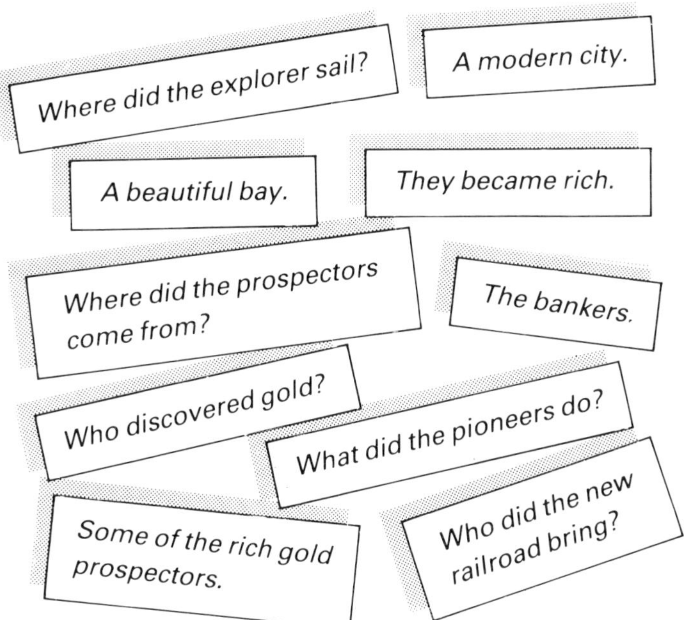

▲ STUDENT A

In pairs, ask and answer questions about the story. For example, Student **A** has:
Where did the explorer sail?

Student **B** has:
Up the coast.

The two sentences make a question and answer. Don't look at your partner's questions or answers.*

▼ STUDENT B

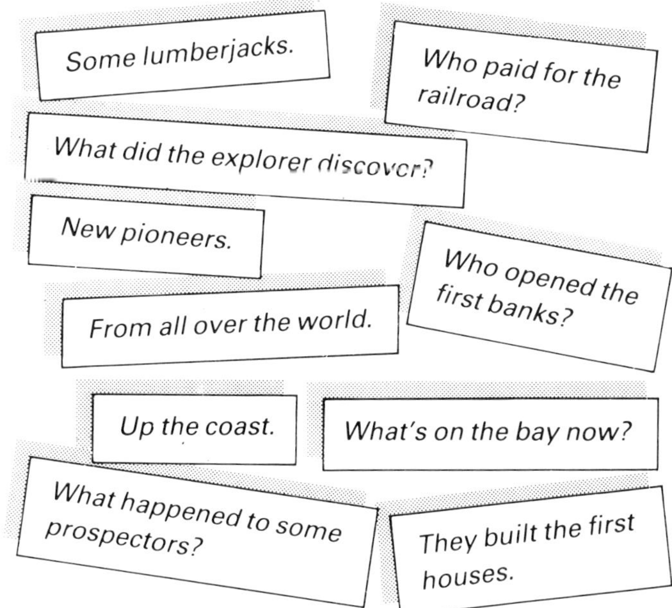

**See Teacher's Manual for alternative presentation.*

Listening and acting out

1

Listen to the cassette and put these pictures (**a–d**) in the correct order in the box below.

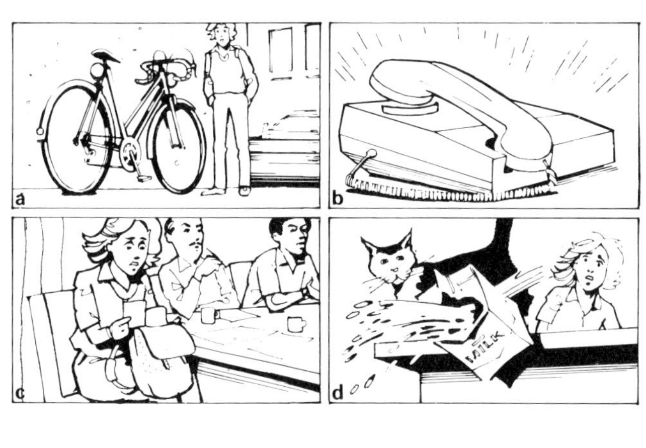

1	2	3	4

2

Answer the questions.

1 Who called?
2 Who knocked over the carton of milk?
3 How did Janet finally get to the meeting?
4 What did she forget?

3

Student **A** arrives late at student **B**'s house. Three things happened to him/her.
Student **B** asks what happened.

Interaction 2

Put the sentences in the correct order to make a dialog. The first one is done for you.*

Interaction 3

Find somebody who/whose:

a has to write letters every day

....

b can sing your favorite song

....

c likes opera music

....

d is going to buy a new pair of shoes next month

....

e takes a subway every day

....

f met a famous person last year

....

g gets up early on Sundays

....

**See Teacher's Manual for alternative presentation.*

Listening and acting out

1

Listen to the cassette and say whether the following statements are true or false.

1 Karen is an athlete.
2 Donna is a marathon runner.
3 Karen doesn't want to make a parachute jump.
4 Donna makes a parachute jump every day.

2

Listen to the cassette again and answer the questions.

1 How often does Karen work out?
2 How far does Karen run every day?
3 When is the marathon race?
4 When is Donna's first jump?

3

In pairs, have a similar conversation. Student **A** invites student **B**.
Student **B** says "No . . . I have to . . ."
Student **A** tries to persuade student **B** (like Donna on the cassette). **B** continues to make excuses.

20

Interaction 1

1 Work in pairs.
2 Write down as much information as you can about another pair of students (full name; family; age; country; likes/dislikes; ambitions; hobbies; responsibilities, etc.).
3 Then interview them to see if you are correct.

Interaction 2

1 Make two teams.
2 Write a different word from Unit 20 in each space below.
3 A member of team A chooses a number from 1–16.
4 A member of team B says his/her word for that number.
5 The member of team A uses that word in a sentence or question. If it's correct, team A gets one point.

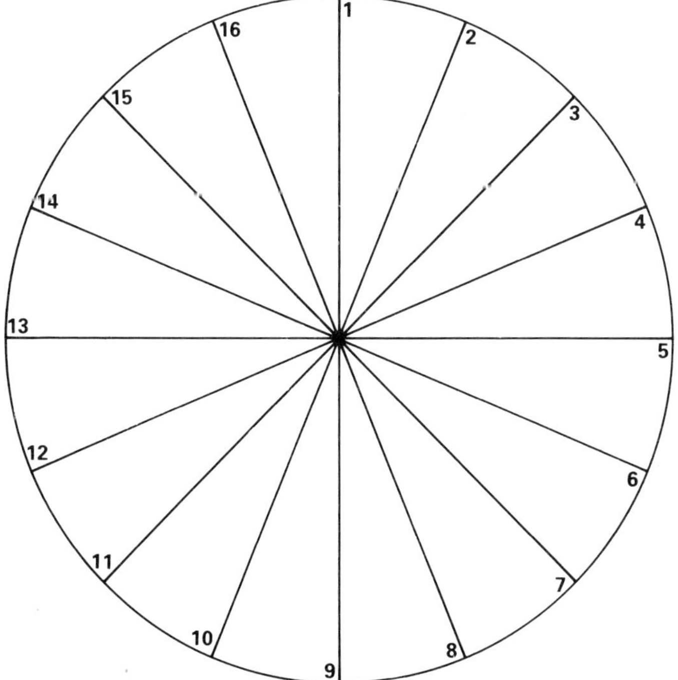

Listening and acting out 

1

Listen to the cassette and fill in the form.

ACE AIRWAYS

LOST/DAMAGED BAGGAGE CLAIM

1 *NAME* ____________________

2 *ADDRESS*
(*local*) ____________________

3 FLIGHT NO.* __________ FROM __________

4 NO. OF BAGS __________ 5 BRAND __________

6 COLOR __________ 7 WEIGHT __________

	IDENTIFICATION TAGS	YES	NO
8	OUTSIDE	☐	☐
9	INSIDE	☐	☐
10	LOCKED	☐	☐

11 CONTENTS
____
____
____

2

Now you have lost something during a flight. Report it to an employee of the airline.

* No. = Number

Grammar summaries and patterns

Note: these do not always follow the order of the units.

BE

Is your	father	a teacher?	Yes, she is. he
	sister	(at)* home?	No, she is not. he

Are your parents at home?	Yes, they are.
Are your friends teachers?	No, they are not.

WAS/WERE

Were you	at home at the bank	yesterday afternoon?	Yes, I was.
			No, I was not.

Where	were you was your mother	on	Monday morning? Tuesday afternoon?	I She	was	at	home. the office.

*In the case of *at home*, the *at* is often omitted.

LOCATION

Where is	the	bank? post office? drugstore?	It's on Union Avenue,	next to across the street from between the bank and	the grocery store.

NATIONALITY

Where	is Pedro are Atsuko and Fumiko	from?	He is They are	from	Mexico. He is Japan. They are	Mexican. Japanese.

DESCRIPTION

How old	is	Carmen?	She	is	twenty-one.
	are	you?	I	am	thirty-two.

When is your birthday?	October thirty-first. April thirtieth.

What color What color	is Pedro's hair? are Sylvie's eyes?	It is They are	brown. blue.

What does	Peter's mother your father	look like?	She He	is	short tall	with	long hair. blue eyes and white hair.

What is	Spaghetti Bolognese? Ratatouille?	It is	an Italian a French	dish with	ground beef, tomatoes eggplant, zucchini, tomatoes	and	onions.

POSSESSION + THIS/THAT/THESE/THOSE

Whose	shoes	are	these? those?	They are	Carmen's.
	tie	is	this? that?	It is	Miguel's.

Are	these yours? those his?	Yes,	they are	mine. his.
Is	this hers? that ours?		it is	hers. ours.

TIME

What time is it?	It is	one two	o'clock. thirty.		
		a quarter		after	one. ten. three.
		three twenty-two	(minutes)		
		a quarter		to	four. six. eleven.
		five fourteen	(minutes)		

PRESENT SIMPLE

Where	do you	live?	In San Diego.	
	does she			
What	do you	do?	I am	an actor.
	does he		He is	

What	do	you	do	in the evenings?	I (usually) go out.
How			get	to work?	by car/bus/subway.
How often	does	she		play tennis?	Twice a week.
What time		he		have dinner?	At nine o'clock.

Do	you they we	like steak?	Yes,	you they we	do.
Does	she he			she he	does.

How often do you	play? go to the movies?	About	twice three times	a	week. month.

What	does	Simon she	do	on	Sundays?	He She	always usually	has lunch at home. goes swimming.
	do	they you			Mondays?	They I	sometimes never	watch TV. get up early.

HAVE

Do	you we they	have the number?	Yes,	I we they	do.	
				she he	does.	
Does	she he		No,	I we they	do	not.
				she he	does	

We don't have any	cookies, bagels, peaches,	but we have some	donuts. oranges. apples.

ABILITY & POSSIBILITY — *CAN/CAN'T*

Can	Lisa Rick and Mary	cook? swim?	Yes,	she they	can.
			No,	she they	can not.

Where can I	buy a nice hat? see a good exhibition?	You can try	the Mad Hatter. the Asian Art Museum.

PRESENT CONTINUOUS

What	is	Sofia your friend	doing?	She He	is	making coffee. tasting a sauce.
	are	you		I	am	frying the onions.
		Rick and Mary		They	are	peeling potatoes.

Is she he	visiting a patient acting	right now?	Yes,	she he	is.	
				they are.		
Are they	studying		No,	she he	is	not.
				they	are	

THERE IS/THERE ARE + COUNT AND MASS NOUNS AND EXPRESSIONS

Count Nouns

Are there any	lakes rivers airports	in Napa Valley?	Yes, there	is one.
				are two.
			No, there are not.	

How many	mushrooms tomatoes potatoes	are there?	There are	a lot. not many. not any.

Mass Nouns

Is there any	oil coal pasture land	in Sonoma valley?	Yes,	there is.
			No,	there is not.

How much	meat milk ketchup	is there?	There is	a lot. not much. not any.

"GOING TO" FUTURE

What	is	Carmen	going to do	in October?	She is	going to	buy an apartment.
	are	Carmen and Miguel you		tomorrow? next week?	They are I am		visit Italy. fly to Buenos Aires.

Why is	Bud Carmen Sylvie	wearing	shorts? a leotard? a ski jacket?	Because	he she	is going to	play tennis. exercise. go skiing.

Are you	going to	take a walk?	Yes,	I am. she is. they are.	
Is she		pass by the drugstore?	No,	I am she is they are	not.

PAST SIMPLE

What did	Sofia you	do	on Monday morning? yesterday?	She I	went	shopping. to the bank.
	Rick and Mary		last Sunday?	They	watched	TV.

Did	Lisa we you	read a medical journal watch TV visit Paris	on Saturday? last night? last year?	Yes,	she we I	did.
				No,	she we I	did not.

Who	composed	West Side Story?	Leonard Bernstein.
	wrote	The Grapes of Wrath?	John Steinbeck.
	invented	the telephone?	Alexander Graham Bell.

When was he born?	In	1451.
When did he die?		1506.

Why is	Christopher Columbus	famous?	Because he	discovered America.
	Buster Keaton			acted in silent movies.

HAVE TO/WANT TO/WOULD LIKE TO

What	does Diane do you	have to do at	work? school?	She has I have	to	type letters. do my homework.

What would	Diane you the girls	like to do?	She I they	would like to	travel round the world. meet interesting people. study philosophy.

He She	has to	go out,	but	he she	doesn't want to	get wet.
		cook the dinner,				miss the movie.
		call home,				have a big bill.

TAG QUESTIONS

Bud	is American,	isn't he?
	can speak Spanish,	can't he?
	lost his dog,	didn't he?
You like spaghetti,		don't you?
They are going to fly to Brazil,		aren't they?

"NEGATIVE" QUESTIONS

Why	didn't	Sylvie	take any photos?	Because	she	dropped her camera.
	can't		lie in the sun?			is sunburned.
	isn't		going to watch TV?		the TV is broken.	

Longman Group UK Limited,
*Longman House, Burnt Mill, Harlow,
Essex CM20 2JE, England
and Associated Companies throughout the world.*

First published 1987

Published in the United States of America by Longman Inc., New York

Library of Congress Cataloging-in-Publication Data

Harmer, Jeremy.
Coast to coast: student's book 1.

1. Readers — 1950– . 2. English language–Text-books for foreign speakers. I. Surguine, Harold. II. Title.
[PE1126.A4H37 1986] 428.6′4 85–23814

ISBN 0-582-90728-4

Produced by Longman Group (FE) Ltd
Printed in Hong Kong

Illustrated by Andrew Aloof and Associates, Fred Apps, Tony Kenyon, Jerry Collins, Malcolm Kemp, Michael Parr, David Parkins, Charles Front

Acknowledgements

We would like to thank the following people for their help and advice during the preparation of *Coast to Coast 1*: Virginia Lo Castro of Simul Academy/Tsukuba University, Tokyo; Terry Tomscha of International House; Nicole Kahan of Pigier Langues, Paris; Karen Davy, Margot Kadesch, and Russel and Beverley Avery. We are also very much obliged to the staff and students at ISSEC in Cergy-Pontoise for their helpful remarks.

We are grateful to the following for permission to reproduce copyright material:

Capper's Weekly for a joke by Julio Kaye, originally published in *Capper's Weekly* June 7, 1983; Sidgwick & Jackson Ltd and Bantam Books Inc. for an adapted extract from *Iacocca: An Autobiography* by Lee Iacocca with William Novak. Copyright © 1984 by Lee Iacocca.

We have unfortunately been unable to trace the copyright holder of an adapted extract about Henry Ford from *The Reader's Digest* April 1985, and would appreciate any information that would enable us to do so.

We are grateful to the following for permission to reproduce copyright photographs:

Asian Art Museum of San Francisco, Golden Gate Park, San Francisco, California for page 37 (bottom); Jim Balog/Black Star for page 49 (right); Ron Sanford/Black Star for page 49 (left); The J. Allan Cash Photolibrary for page 71 (top); Clive Barda Photography for page 15 (right); The Image Bank for page 37 (top); Philip Prosen/The Image Bank for page 65; Peter Newark's Western Americana for page 31; The Photo Source for page 63; Lou Jones/Uniphoto for page 35; photo courtesy of Woodcliff Lake Hilton, Woodcliff Lake, NJ for page 22 (top); Zefa for pages 33 and 71 (bottom).
Cover photograph by G. Brimacombe/The Image Bank.
All photographs not listed above were taken by Con Putbrace.